For a New
International De

Angelos Th. Angelopoulos

foreword by
Guido Carli

The Praeger Special Studies program—
utilizing the most modern and efficient book
production techniques and a selective
worldwide distribution network—makes
available to the academic, government, and
business communities significant, timely
research in U.S. and international economic, social, and political development.

For a New Policy of International Development

PRAEGER SPECIAL STUDIES IN INTERNATIONAL ECONOMICS AND DEVELOPMENT

Praeger Publishers   New York   London

Library of Congress Cataloging in Publication Data

Angelopoulos, Angelos Theodorou, 1904-
    For a new policy of international development.

    (Praeger special studies in international economics
and development)
    Translation of Pour une nouvelle politique du
development international.
    1. Economic history—1945-   2. Economic
policy.   3. International economic relations.
I. Title.
HC59.A79413   1977   338.91   77-24420
ISBN 0-03-022816-6
ISBN 0-03-022821-2 student ed.

Originally published in French as *Pour une nouvelle politique
du dévelopment international.*
©1976, Presses Universitaires de France

PRAEGER SPECIAL STUDIES
200 Park Avenue, New York, N.Y., 10017, U.S.A.

Published in the United States of America in 1977
by Praeger Publishers,
A Division of Holt, Rinehart and Winston, CBS, Inc.

789   038   987654321

English translation © 1977 by Praeger Publishers

Printed in the United States of America

In recent years numerous assessments of the causes of the current economic crisis have been presented to the public by eminent economists, politicians, and observers of economic affairs. Indeed, there has been no dearth of theories attempting to identify "the" causes and "the" solutions to our present problems. On the other hand, there appears to have been an inverse correlation between the quantity of such solutions and the improvement of actual economic affairs. The public may well be skeptical of another book on the same subject.

However, this volume merits the close attention of readers from all backgrounds for it is unique in several important respects. First, most of the previous analyses have been written from the point of view of the effects of the crisis on a particular country. They have thus tended to reflect the goals and expectations of the inhabitants of that country. Angelos Th. Angelopoulos, who is governor of the National Bank of Greece, does not adopt this approach, but rather draws on his wide experience in international affairs to emphasize that the current crisis is, in fact, worldwide in both its nature and its influence. He argues forcefully that it can only be analyzed from the point of view of international economic relationships.

This recognition of the ever-increasing interdependence of the economic systems of the world produces an analysis of the utmost importance, especially for readers in the more industrialized countries. The author points out that, while the recent process of inflation with rising unemployment and stagnant growth has had very undesirable and uncomfortable effects on the industrialized countries, the effects have been minimal compared with those suffered by the lesser developed countries, in particular the poorest, which has a population of over 1 billion and a per capita income of less than $200 per year. In fact, Professor Angelopoulos shows how the crisis has created structural relations that have had a differentially more severe impact on these countries. This differential impact on the developing world (excluding, of course, the petroleum producing countries) may be the single most important aspect of the worldwide crisis—yet it has received only minor attention.

One can only agree with the author's judgment on the importance of these effects

> when one sees how much of the world's resources remain unused, how many needs of the world's population remain unsatisfied, how many millions or rather hundreds of millions there are who do not find work and who increase the number of the unemployed. This, at a time when the scientific and technological progress of our epoch can ensure on a worldwide scale the productive use of all these factors through rational, planned policies conceived so as to accelerate economic progress and prosperity for humanity as a whole.

Given the pervasiveness of the phenomena of the crisis and its particularly direct impact on the developing world, can the causes of these conditions also be identified as worldwide in nature? The author's response to this question is that "the underlying cause of inflation and unemployment is, in the first instance, the insufficiency of productive investments. This insufficiency has the direct result of diminishing the supply of goods and services available to satisfy demand. From this originate inflation and unemployment, as a consequence of the nonsatisfaction of overall demand."

In identifying the role of "productive investment" as the motive force of the expansion of supply, Professor Angelopoulos also makes an interesting contribution to the current debate among academic economists concerning the applicability of orthodox Keynesian theory and policy to the analysis and cure of the current dilemma, or as some call it, paradox, of inflation with unemployment, by suggesting that the basic method of approach is sound, but that it must recognize that

> the technological progress of our times has created new conditions that require an enlargement of the Keynesian theory. New conditions in the labor market, the social policy adopted with respect to the unemployed, the environment, pollution, the confirmed widening of the gap between rich and poor countries, polycentrism in international politics—all these factors require new ways of looking at and thinking about economic and social problems. These have now become world problems.

Thus the causes are as pervasive as the effects that support the main theme of the book, namely, that since the problems and causes of the current conditions are worldwide, their solution must be based on a worldwide analysis of the problem. "Under present conditions, when each industrial country finds itself in a vicious circle of inflation and unemployment, no single country can in fact through its own policy resolve the problem of the crisis or create a sustained growth. It is possible that the policy of full employment in the industrialized countries has reached and even surpassed the limits of application."

To paraphrase a well-known saying, it is no longer possible to have "full employment in one country," or even in one small group of countries. Full employment and stable growth can only be achieved by creating the organizations and international institutions capable of generating sufficient productive investment on a world-wide scale. Furthermore, this process must have as its starting point investment in the countries of the lesser developed world.

Given the existing degree of economic interdependence and interpenetration it is no longer possible for one country to act independently of the rest of the world. Nor is it any longer possible for the industrialized countries to act as a group independently of the rest of the world; indeed, it is not even in their best interest to do so.

Because the economic crisis is at present widespread and affects all countries, the remedial policies that should be applied must also be extended globally to cover the totality of the countries of the world. Seen from this angle, an increased demand that could stimulate large investments in the industrialized countries would especially come from the countries of the Third World and particularly from the poorest countries.

The specific proposals made by the author for the creation of new global institutions and the strengthening of existing organizations and institutions to this end, some of which have already inspired changes in international economic policy, have the merit of providing specific points of reference in the discussion of the factors of crucial importance that are outlined in this book. It is notoriously difficult to attain agreement on even the simplest matters when international affairs are under discussion. The same will certainly be true of the specific proposals advanced here. Even if they are not adopted, they will have served their purpose if they can direct the analysis of current economic affairs beyond national borders and beyond the effects on the rates of growth of the industrialized countries toward consideration of international influences and the impact on the Third World where the future of the growth and development of the industrialized countries will be decided.

The world economy is undergoing a profound and generalized crisis, and its future is open to question. Is this a crisis that will pass? What are the causes? Why do inflation and unemployment take place? What are the prospects for ending the crisis? What should be the shape of a new international development policy? In the framework of this new strategy, what role should investments play on a world scale? How can the surplus of petrodollars and the increase in the value of gold be used? What is the true meaning of "the new international economic order"?

These are the questions that will be the subject of this book. In my book *The Third World and the Rich Countries* (1972), I expressed uneasiness about the future of the world economy and emphasized that, if appropriate measures were not taken in time, an economic recession of international scope would become inevitable.

Developments in 1974 and 1975 confirmed this forecast. The spectacular increase in the price of oil has clearly revealed the structural weaknesses of the economic system and the irrationality in the functioning of the world economy. The slight economic recovery in 1976 was slow and fragile, and prospects for the coming years are not encouraging.

The failure of the international conferences and summits held to consider these questions, and the difficulties in the North-South dialogue that has been under way in Paris, demonstrate that no single country or group of countries can bring about effective solutions to the present crisis.

A radical change in ways of looking at the great problems of our epoch is more necessary than ever. A fundamental reform in the structures and institutions of the economic system is indispensable. Only an international development strategy capable of establishing a new world economic order—the main features of which are indicated in this book—could contribute to economic and social progress and ensure world peace.

The proposals we put forward are based on the idea of international solidarity, on the conviction that there is a collective task in which all countries and all peoples must participate. This presupposes that the industrialized countries, including the socialist countries, become conscious of their responsibility toward other countries and speedily adopt a new international development policy. Otherwise, the economic, social, and political situation will continue to deteriorate. In fact, studies by various international bodies conclude that prospects until the end of the century are not at all bright. In the best of circumstances the Western economies must learn to live with persistent inflation, high unemployment, and growth rates lower than in the 1950s and 1960s. Meanwhile the gap between rich and poor countries remains dangerously large and poverty threatens to lead to world social and political revolution.

CONTENTS

LIST OF TABLES AND FIGURES

After a long period of exceptional growth, the Western econ-omies entered a new phase in the beginning of 1974, a phase that has brought profound changes in the international system. Gen-eralized recession, high inflation, increasing and disturbing unem-ployment, declining industrial production and national income, an unprecedented rise in balance-of-payments deficits—these are the characteristic problems in this new situation. To these should be added the bankruptcy of the gold-exchange standard, the system established at Bretton Woods, a development that has shaken the international monetary system.

FROM PROSPERITY TO RECESSION

This rapid transition from increasing poverty to stagflation whose effects are worldwide was a shock for the industrialized countries of the Western bloc, a striking example of a rupture of equilibrium in economic history. Although the developed coun-tries had experienced phases of economic slowdown between 1945 and 1975, these never reached the point of so deep and generalized a recession. Despite occasional indications to the contrary, govern-ments had been convinced that economic progress would continue without great disturbances, or at least would always be under con-trol.

The International Development Strategy adopted on October 24, 1970, by the General Assembly of the United Nations, fore-saw for 1970–80 an average rate of growth of 6 percent annually for all the developed and developing countries, and was based on a confident view of the future. And the Western industrialized world showed little awareness of the consequences that could flow from an eventual recession. Even in 1974, although eco-nomic activity as a whole showed some early signs of weakness, the governments primarily concerned—and, even more surpris-ingly, the numerous forecasting studies by international organiza-tions and the private sector—made no mention of what the 1975 *Annual Report* of the International Monetary Fund would term "the extent of weakness in real activity and strength in price pressures."

Undoubtedly, one of the most striking features of this evolution toward general stagflation was the increase in the price of crude oil, a price that after a long period of relative stability more than quadrupled after October 1973. This sudden increase not only led to a rise in domestic prices but also brought about a significant deterioration of foreign trade balances. The industrial countries whose commercial balances were until then in surplus now showed deficits, and an unbalancing of international economic and monetary equilibrium began.

However, it must be recognized that the increase in the price of oil instituted by OPEC (Organization of Petroleum Exporting Countries) was not the only cause of the economic disorder. This unprecedented readjustment only reinforced the influence of several factors that had begun to provoke inflationary effects. It brought into the open pre-existing problems and contradictions that had already created great disturbances in the functioning of the economy.

The size and intensity of these economic disruptions and the short- and long-term problems they posed did not receive sufficient attention from governments. But the shock of the abrupt increase in oil prices put them face to face with reality.

DILEMMAS FACING GOVERNMENTS

During 1976, despite encouraging signs of recovery in some industrialized countries, the prospects for the future appeared poor and doubtful. Moreover, the monetary crisis—which during the first quarter again created a climate of uncertainty in exchange rates—now threatened all the European economies and threatened to wipe out any indications of slight recovery and renewed confidence.

This situation further deteriorated because the governments of the industrialized countries had to deal with two problems whose solutions were diametrically opposed. They had either to take measures against inflation, and risk aggravating the recession and increasing unemployment, or alternatively to stimulate employment and revive economic activity and thereby risk accentuating inflationary pressures. Thus, in the middle of the 1970s the developed countries were experiencing an extraordinary and unprecedented combination of inflation and recession that appeared to endanger the foundations of their economic and social systems and indeed that of society as a whole.

One obstacle that prevented the adoption of a positive and effective policy to overcome the crisis was the lack of cooperation among world leaders. In spite of repeated summits and meetings between representatives of the large industrialized countries, no progress had been made toward the adoption and application of a global policy capable of contributing to economic recovery on a worldwide scale.

The same lack of coordination could be noted on the part of the oil-producing countries. They were not able to conceive or carry out their role in a global perspective. Surprised by an accumulation of unbounded wealth, they were living in a climate of permanent suspicion toward the industrial world—a suspicion that undoubtedly resulted from their long experience of exploitation of natural resources by foreign companies that had abused the privileges given them.

These countries were beginning to devote a limited part of their income to the developing countries, but they also followed a hesitant policy. They were seeking the way that best suited them to play a more important role on the international scene and in the world economy.

The rest of the world—that is, the countries of the Third World that are not oil producers, which represent three-fourths of the population of our planet—were the major victims of this international disequilibrium. In fact, the economic crisis has affected the developing countries most, especially the poorest among them.

THE SCANDAL OF THE CRISIS

These developments occurred at a time when responsible statesmen and the United Nations were speaking of the need to undertake "a global policy" favoring progress and prosperity in the world. However, these same leaders were not able to agree on such an overall policy. This is the scandal of the crisis.

It is indeed an intolerable scandal when one sees how much of the world's resources remain unused, how many needs of the world's population remain unsatisfied, how many millions or rather hundreds of millions do not find work and swell the ranks of the unemployed. This, at a time when scientific and technological progress can ensure on a worldwide scale the productive use of all these factors through rational, planned policies conceived so as to accelerate economic progress and prosperity for humanity as a whole.

We thus live in the midst of a crisis that, even though it does not resemble the great crisis of the 1930s, takes on the character of a crisis of civilization. For to the economic and monetary crisis has now been added the crisis of power—political crises, civil wars, problems of pollution and environment, acts of anarchy and terrorism; these inevitably create general disorder and introduce uncertainties that make it necessary to pose the question of the future of the world.

Consequently, it would appear urgent to reexamine our methods of thinking and to reconsider, in a new way, the totality of the vast problems of our epoch, taking into account the permanently evolving conditions of economic and social life.

A HISTORICAL ERROR

Gold and oil provide characteristic examples of the need for a permanent readjustment of policy objectives to new conditions. These commodities play a major role in the functioning of our economic and monetary system. History has shown that if adjustments in the price of a product are not made and a stable price is maintained too long despite market conditions, eventually there will be a sudden price increase. The repercussions will be all the greater if the role of this product is economically important. Is this not what has happened with respect to gold? The stability of the gold price, maintained without change for more than 35 years on the basis of the relevant international agreements, has been one of the main causes of disorder in the international monetary system. If the price of gold had been readjusted after 1965 and aligned to prices of other goods, speculation would have been eliminated and the monetary situation today would be very different.

The same phenomenon can be seen, with certain nuances, in the case of oil. In fact, the price of oil was maintained too long without change. Moreover, the policy of maintaining the price of oil at low levels discouraged the search for other energy resources and encouraged waste. The Yom Kippur war was a politically motivated pretext to begin to bring about a sharp increase in oil prices. This explains why the increase went beyond the level justified by general price increases.

The attitude of the industrialized countries, in wanting to keep the price of oil too low for a long time, was a primary cause of the disruption in the world economy. The resulting disorder made clear other economic and social factors, and even posed basic questions about the foundations of the existing economic system. The Western world thus preferred to underscore the increase of crude oil prices—even though the effects of the oil price increase on all the industrial and agricultural sectors combined was, as we shall see further on, less important than expected—rather than to face reality.

These manifestations of a new will on the part of the oil-producing and basic materials-producing countries must now be taken into account. For this change marks the beginning of a new development policy that may lead to a fundamental shift in the geopolitical map.

THE NEED FOR A NEW POLICY

Clearly the international administrative apparatus that has been managing the world's resources does not seem able to resolve the great problems of our epoch. Consequently, profound structural changes in the economy and society are needed to establish a new international economic order and, in a spirit of social justice and worldwide solidarity, to adopt a new policy based on an equitable distribution of income and wealth among all countries.

This new international economic order, which was the main subject of the Seventh Special Session of the United Nations General Assembly (September 1975) and was adopted as a principle by that body, constitutes a historic step forward. Its importance must not be underestimated.

The industrialized countries have every reason to engage in interstate discussions, based on a recognition of the convergence of reciprocal interests, aimed at reaching a worldwide agreement on solving the great economic and social problems—which become more alarming each day. To ignore the need for such a policy can only endanger world peace. Let us not forget that the political power of the developing countries is increasing from day to day. By the end of this century 83 out of every 100 active inhabitants of the globe will live in regions now considered underdeveloped. Moreover, of the 144 states represented in the United Nations General Assembly the Western industrialized countries account for only a maximum of 25. The 108 developing countries, which represent 3 billion persons, are trying to join together in all fields to exert growing political and moral pressure. To ignore or underestimate this situation is to risk abrupt institutional changes.

A new international development policy requires a concrete and effective program to develop world resources, which should be considered the patrimony of humanity as a whole. That is the guiding purpose of this study. For only a policy that coordinates goals and practical measures for the application of a new development strategy—as defined in this book—can contribute to recovery and sustained world economic growth.

The present crisis, which challenges established values and prevailing doctrines, should help us in the search for the radical reforms needed by the present system—reforms that could not be put into effect during a period of sustained economic growth.

The future will depend in large part on the capacity of the leaders of all countries—the industrialized countries, the socialist countries, the oil-producing countries, and the developing countries—to appreciate the gravity and complexity of these problems and to reach consensus on a global plan to deal with them. The success of such a policy will depend above all on the effectiveness of the United Nations. Overcoming its present apathy and adapting itself to the needs of the new situation, this organization again should take up the constructive role defined in its charter: to ensure progress, welfare, and world peace.

For a New Policy of International Development

1

THE OIL PROBLEM AND THE STRUCTURAL WEAKNESSES OF THE ECONOMIC SYSTEM

THE REPERCUSSIONS OF THE OIL CRISIS

The abrupt increase in oil prices since January 1974 is, as indicated in the Introduction, one of the most powerful causes of the present international recession (see Figure 1.1). This recession is accompanied by a loss of equilibrium in the balances of payments of most countries and of the general international economic and monetary order.

However, it must be recognized that the increase in oil prices determined by OPEC (the Organization of Petroleum Exporting Countries) was not the only cause of economic disorder.[1] This price reevaluation reinforced the influence of many factors that already had begun to provoke inflationary effects. Indeed, since 1972 the more rapid increase in global demand than in supplies, especially

---

1. OPEC (Organization of Petroleum Exporting Countries) was established in Bagdad in September 1960 by Saudi Arabia, Iraq, Iran, Kuwait, and Venezuela. Eight countries have since joined: Qatar (1961), Libya (1962), Indonesia, Dhabi (1967), Algeria (1969), Nigeria (1971), Ecuador (1973), and Gabon (1975). The United Kingdom expects to join OPEC when it begins to export oil from the North Sea.

FIGURE 1.1
Evolution of Crude Oil Prices
(in U.S. dollars per barrel)

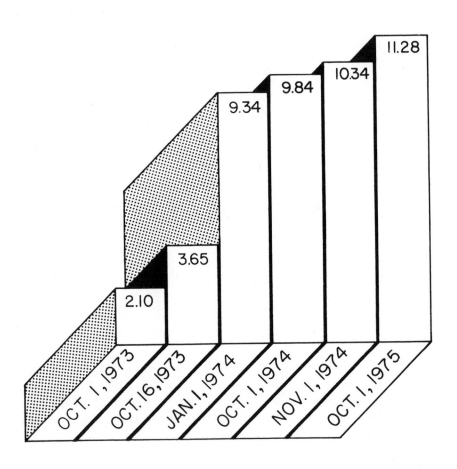

*Saudi Arabia and the Gulf Emirates increased their prices on January 1, 1977, by 5 percent. All other OPEC countries increased by 10 percent and indicated that a further 5 percent increase would be introduced in July 1977.

Source: L'Economie, January 27, 1976.

of foodstuffs and certain basic industrial products, had engendered a wage and price spiral; this was accentuated by the increase in oil prices. Furthermore, various developments during 1970–76, including the priority given to irrational and unproductive investments for rearmament and the conquest of space, had exceptionally serious repercussions on the world economy.

The impact of the oil price increase on the totality of industrial and agricultural sectors has been less than expected. According to International Monetary Fund (IMF) estimates, the effect of the reevaluation of crude oil prices on costs of production is relatively small—about 2 percent. Also, according to a study by the Organization for Economic Cooperation and Development (OECD), "the negative effect of the energy crisis on the supply capacity needed for economic expansion, short, medium and long-term, will probably not be very great."[2] In the opinion of an OECD working group, "the loss of potential production represents less than 1 percent of GNP, in virtually all the member countries."

There undoubtedly have been very unfavorable repercussions on products with a high energy content, but it is important not to exaggerate the overall consequences. This view coincides with the conclusions of a study prepared for a private research center, the Brookings Institution of Washington, D.C.[3] This study states that although the abrupt oil price increase was a severe shock for all industrialized countries in 1974 and 1975, its long-term consequences will not be great and will not affect growth or living standards.

Table 1.1 shows that for 1974 the direct incidence of the increased oil prices on price levels in OECD countries can be estimated at 3.5 percent. About one half this amount (1.8 percent) corresponds to the increase in the cost of net oil imports and the other half to the increased price of energy from domestic sources.

It is difficult to measure the indirect effects of the oil price increases. According to OECD estimates, the multiplier is close to two. In other words, a 1 percent price rise would lead to a subsequent wage increase that would add another 1 percent to the increase of the general price level.

---

2. See Report of OECD Working Group No. 2, February 13, 1975, Chateau de la Muette, Paris.

3. Brookings Institution, *Higher Oil Prices and the World Economy* (Washington, D.C., 1975).

TABLE 1.1

Incidence of the Increase in the Price of Oil, 1973 and 1974

	In the OECD Countries	In the Non-Oil-Producing Developing Countries
Increase in the cost of oil imports[a]		
Billions of dollars	64.0	11.0
Percent of GNP 1974	1.8	1.6
Real increase in OPEC exports in 1974		
Billions of dollars	20.0	1.8
Percent of GNP 1974	0.6	0.3
Direct deflationary incidence[b]		
Percent of GNP 1974	1.2	1.3
Contribution to cost inflation (percent of the index of prices derived from GNP)		
Direct incidence of the increased cost of oil	1.8	1.6
Direct incidence including the increased price of domestic energy supplies	3.5	—

[a]Equivalent to a transfer of real income to the OPEC countries.

[b]Share in GNP of the increase in the cost of oil imports in 1973-74 less the portion of GNP resulting from the increase in exports to OPEC in 1973-74, representing the unexpended receipts of OPEC as a percentage of the GNP of the two groups of oil importing countries.

Source: OECD secretariat, April 1976.

It would therefore be an exaggeration to see the increase of oil prices as the main cause of inflation and to contend that "a lower oil price would make possible more rapid economic recovery around the world."[4] But the industrialized countries have preferred, as we have indicated, to pay more attention to the increase in oil prices than to seeking the real cause of the crisis. In this way, they have been able conveniently to cover up their own mistakes in economic and social policy.

We probably would have equally strong inflation and equally disquieting unemployment, even without the quadrupling of oil prices. The oil price increase was only the accelerator that revealed the structural weaknesses of the economic system. This system, although it utilizes incomparable techniques for business cycle analyses and forecasting, has not succeeded in using these techniques effectively to lead the economy of today—an economy that Alfred Sauvy has termed "devilish"—out of the impasse.

The driving force of the increase in oil prices made 1974 the international year of excessive inflation, which inevitably brought about and will continue to engender grave problems of economic and monetary policy.

Although the price formation process is complex and it is impossible to identify or isolate the secondary effects of an external shock, it must be recognized that the increase in the oil price provided a new element that stimulated anticipations of inflation and created very important psychological effects. According to OECD estimates, the direct and indirect effects could be on the order of 6 to 8 percent. Undoubtedly this influenced the 1974 rate of inflation, which reached an unprecedented 14.5 percent in the industrialized countries.

Today the extent of the grave world crisis does not permit illusions about a spectacular economic recovery. Let us remember that at the end of 1974 governments foresaw a rapid economic recovery that did not take place. During 1975 international organizations frequently presented optimistic forecasts—and later discounted

---

4. At the North-South Conference of December 1975, held in Paris, U.S. Secretary of State Henry Kissinger said in his inaugural address: "The abrupt and arbitrary increase in the price of oil has been one of the principal factors contributing to rates of inflation and unemployment unprecedented since the 1930s." He added: "A lower oil price would have permitted the acceleration of the recovery of the world economy." See *Le Monde*, December 18, 1975.

them as erroneous. In fact, from an economic viewpoint 1975 was the worst peacetime year since World War II.[5] The year 1976 brought only a small improvement, and for 1977 no significant reduction of inflation or unemployment is foreseen.

Against the background of this dark horizon, each country is waiting for its economy to be reactivated by an induction effect derived from recovery plans initiated by its partner countries. Confronted with this ambiguity, private firms hesitate to undertake investments while governments, for fear of spurring inflation, do not adopt the stimulative measures they could take.

THE SEVERE EFFECTS ON
THE DEVELOPING COUNTRIES

The developing countries—the Third World—have suffered the most severe effects of this international disequilibrium.[6] The structural weaknesses that characterize their economies increase their dependence on the outside world. The less a country is developed, the more its development depends on the action of the rich countries and on external events. By contrast, the more a country is developed, the more capable it is of taking steps to overcome economic and monetary difficulties. Thus, the inflationary and

---

5. On the evolution of the economy in 1975, see "The Economic and Social Year 1975," *Le Monde* (Paris, 1976); "The Economic Perspectives for 1976," *OECD Observer*, November-December 1975; Alfred Sauvy, *L'Economie du diable: Chômage et inflation* (Paris: Calmann-Levy, 1976); M. Mesarovic and E. Pestel, *Stratégie pour demain* (Paris: Le Seuil, 1974); P. Heymann and B. Berteloot, *Aujourd'hui et demain: La crise* (Paris: Clattés, 1974); Sisco Mansholt, *La Crise* (Paris: Stock, 1974); *L'Emploi, la croissance et les besoins essentiels* (Geneva: Bureau International de Travail, 1976); J. W. Howe, *The U.S. and World Development* (New York: Praeger, 1975).

6. On this subject, see Angelos Angelopoulos, *The Third World and the Rich Countries: Perspectives for the Year 2000* (New York: Praeger, 1973). Also see Gunnar Myrdal, *Asian Drama: An Inquiry into the Poverty of Nations* (New York: Pantheon, 1968), 3 vols.

recessionary effects of recent developments have more particularly affected the developing economies.[7]

In addition, the harmful effect of the increase of oil prices has been amplified for the developing countries: (1) by the continuous increase of prices of industrial products imported from the rich countries and (2) by the fact that they have received little or no benefit from development aid provided through "recycling" of petrodollar surpluses from the OPEC countries.

It also should be noted that these unfavorable effects have coincided with a large decline in the prices of basic materials and agricultural products; before 1973 these prices had significantly improved the payments balances of developing countries producing such goods. The increase in oil prices and the deep recession in the industrialized countries have caused unfavorable supplementary effects that brought about a 1975 deficit of about $35 billion in the current balance of payments of the developing countries. This deficit is four times greater than the deficit of $9 billion incurred in 1973, that is, before the increase in the price of oil.

The deterioration of the terms of trade of the developing countries has contributed greatly to this situation. In 1974 and 1975 the prices of their imports increased by 40 percent while their export prices only increased by 27 percent. Another aggravating factor is the decrease in the volume of the developing countries' exports—a result of the persistent recession in the industrialized countries, which normally absorb 75 percent of their exports. For the poorest countries in particular, where per capita income is less than $200 and population totals 1 billion persons, the situation is even more serious.

It may however be said that during the first four years of the United Nations' "Second Development Decade" the developing countries made satisfactory progress by achieving an average rate of growth of about 6 percent annually. On the other hand, the deterioration in their terms of trade, following the recession in the

---

7. William Cline, *International Monetary Reform and the Developing Countries* (Washington: Brookings Institution, 1976).

developed countries and the abrupt increase in oil prices, has brought them to a critical point. The insufficiency of public development assistance has greatly contributed to this. Such assistance only reached half the objective established by the United Nations, that is, 0.36 percent of the gross national product (GNP) in 1975 instead of 0.70 percent. As a result, the total transfers of resources (loans, investments, and official contributions)—which in reality as we have indicated in another study[8] does not constitute aid but rather financing on unfavorable terms—has amounted to only 0.8 percent of GNP, a figure significantly less than the objective of 1 percent established by the United Nations.

According to a recent United Nations study, all these factors have engendered "a general feeling of disappointment and frustration."[9] It was for this reason that at the Paris North-South Conference, in which 27 countries participated (industrialized countries, countries newly enriched through oil, and the disinherited countries of the Third World), the representatives of the developing countries came with mixed feelings of doubt, suspicion, and faith—but ready to join together to reach an acceptable compromise.[10]

As we shall see later, it is this situation that makes most urgent a decision favoring constructive and dynamic international cooperation.

It is disappointing to note that the fourth UNCTAD (United Nations Conference on Trade and Development), which took

---

8. Angelopoulos, *The Third World and the Rich Countries*, p. 85; and particularly the chapter on "The Myth of Development Assistance."

9. United Nations document E/A.C.62/8 (May 5, 1975).

10. Participants in the Conference on International Economic Cooperation, held in Paris beginning on December 16, 1975 were: the European Economic Community, the United States, Japan, and seven developing countries (Algeria, Saudi Arabia, Brazil, India, Iran, Venezuela, and Zaire). In addition, the industrialized countries and the developing countries designated five industrialized countries and 12 developing countries from their respective groups. As a result the number of participants in the North-South dialogue was 27; the secretary-general of the United Nations also attended as a guest.

place in May 1976 in Nairobi, did not bring about concrete results. After 20 days of confrontation, a compromise was reached
on one of the subjects under discussion—stabilization of basic
materials prices. This compromise avoided a breakdown of the
conference and left the door open to the creation of a common
fund to support international agreements on basic materials.

On two other subjects—the excessive indebtedness of the
developing countries and transfers of technology from the developed to the developing countries—UNCTAD decided to await
the results of the discussions at the North-South Conference.

For this reason, UNCTAD was only "a simple exchange of
views," and according to a spokesman for the less developed countries was "very disappointing."[11]

THE LACK OF COOPERATION

Adoption of a positive, effective policy to deal with the
present crisis is hindered at least in part by the lack of cooperation among responsible government leaders, particularly among
the industrialized countries which have at their disposal the necessary machinery to tackle today's economic and monetary difficulties. The heads of state in the European community met three times
in 1975—in Dublin (March), Brussels (July), and Rome (December).
Furthermore, the International Monetary Fund and the World
Bank held their sessions in Washington in September 1975 and a
summit meeting took place in Rambouillet in November 1975.[12]
Lastly, mention may be made of the North-South Conference held
in Paris in December 1975, convened to explore the overall problems

---

11. Gamani Corea, secretary-general of UNCTAD, said at a press conference at the 4th session of the UNITAD meeting in Nairobi, Kenya, May
1976, "The results obtained with regard to the debt problem are very slight.
We have not had the concrete results for which we hoped."

12. At the summit conference held November 15-17, 1975, in Rambouillet (near Paris), participants were the heads of state of West Germany,
the United States, France, the United Kingdom, Italy, and Japan.

of the Western world, and the Conference of Puerto Rico held at the end of June 1976.

All these meetings made it possible to analyze the economic situation and international trends, but they did not produce any concrete decisions.

Moreover, the contradictory interests of the industrialized countries have led to an economic antagonism that has contributed to deterioration of international trade and has aggravated the monetary crisis.

The main responsibility falls on the United States, which through its "national" monetary and commercial policy sought above all to protect its own interests. This policy brought about a very rapid improvement in the commercial balance of payments despite the domestic recession in the United States—but without achieving similar results for the international economy as a whole. Indeed, the United States achieved great improvement in its commercial balance as a result of its monetary policy, which lowered costs of production in comparison with other industrialized countries. Thus, the commercial balance changed from a deficit of $3.8 billion for 1974 to a surplus of $8.4 billion for 1975. The lowering of the wage costs in the United States as a result of the successive devaluations of the dollar gave a considerable impetus to American exports.[13]

Table 1.2 shows that in almost all industrialized countries hourly wage costs increased from 77 to 214 percent between 1970 and 1975. But the increase was only 43 percent in the United States. Now, Sweden, Norway, and Canada show higher wage costs than that for the American worker.

Another example of the lack of cooperation among the industrialized countries was the European monetary crisis of March 1976, characterized by the break-up of the monetary "snake." It also is clear from this break-up that the countries of

---

13. In an article criticizing the economic and monetary policy of the United States, the former Prime Minister of France, Michel Debré, emphasized that "the United States sacrificed the monetary order to satisfy its own national imperatives" (see *Le Monde*, July 7, 1976).

TABLE 1.2

Hourly Wage Costs, Including Social Charges
(in U.S. dollars)

	1970	1975	Rate of Increase (percent)
Sweden	$3.01	$7.12	+137
Norway	2.49	6.56	+163
Canada	3.49	6.19	+ 77
United States	4.25	6.06	+ 43
Belgium	2.08	6.05	+191
West Germany	2.43	5.64	+132
Switzerland	1.99	5.03	+153
Italy	1.87	4.36	+133
France	1.74	4.01	+130
United Kingdom	1.68	3.70	+120
Japan	1.10	3.45	+214

Source: Swedish Employers Confederation, reproduced in *U.S. News and World Report*, February 9, 1976.

the European community, as a result of the worsening economic disorder, are not able to apply common monetary and economic policies. This chaotic situation leads each country to seek above all to protect its own interests, using its currency as a weapon of economic warfare.[14] Moreover, protectionist reactions are multiplying throughout the world and a system of tightly controlled and organized international trade is appearing.[15] Even the European Economic Community has increased its external tariffs as a

---

14. See Jacqueline Graphin, "La Guerre economique," *Le Monde*, June 11, 12, and 13, 1976.

15. "We have been witnessing for some time a resurgence of protectionist behavior," declared Raymond Barre, then French minister of foreign trade on June 11, 1976, speaking before the Franco-American Chamber of Commerce. He added, "These protectionist measures tend to be cloaked

measure of economic protection, and this has created additional obstacles for world trade.

Under such conditions, how can we talk of effective and constructive international cooperation? The same lack of cooperation exists among the oil-producing countries. These countries have taken decisions that—even if justified in large measure by increases in prices of industrial products—nevertheless conflicted with the interests of the world community. They have not yet decided to use a significant part of their wealth in a spirit of international solidarity.[16] Nor have they recognized that ignoring the interdependence of national economies can hurt their own interests—as it does now.

A lack of cooperation also exists among the countries of the Third World. At the Manila Conference (February 1976) to discuss the "new economic order," the countries of the "Group of 77" opposed each other on such issues as the enlargement of the generalized system of preferences, tariff advantages, the constitution of reserve stocks of raw materials, and the means of coordination between UNCTAD and the North-South Conference.

It is nevertheless impossible to understand the lack of a global policy to confront a generalized crisis that is spreading to all domains, a crisis that is becoming not only economic and social but also political, and may even be considered a crisis of civilization itself.[17]

This comes at a time when responsible statesmen worry about the need for a common policy toward world problems. Did not

---

behind respectable concerns such as ecology or public health protection." *Bulletin of Franco-American Chamber of Commerce*, Paris.

16. The sum of $1 billion initially approved as aid to the poor countries subsequently was reduced to $800 million.

17. Jacques Attali, in *La parole ou l'Outil* (Paris: PUF, 1975), underlines that the present crisis is also the crisis of this power structure showing increasing signs of confusion. "The man in power, within the enterprise or the State," he writes, "is beginning in fact to sense the unsuitability of the instruments and institutions at his disposal to cope with the present upheaval" (p.

former U.S. Secretary of State Henry Kissinger emphasize* that "the task of the next 25 years will be to construct a global society, the lack of which would mean chaos for all"? French President Valery Giscard d'Estaing has said his policy is based on a "universalization" of problems. Other heads of state also have called for global solutions. Even the Rambouillet meeting recognized the urgent need for an extensive cooperation:

> We have decided to fulfill our responsibilities fully, to develop our efforts aimed at an increased international cooperation and a constructive dialogue among all countries irrespective of the disparities in their economic development, inequality in their resources and differences in the political and social systems.

However, these same statesmen have not been able to agree on a comprehensive policy. This is the scandal of the crisis to which we have referred.[18]

---

14). Also see Bertrand de Jouvenel, *La Civilisation de puissance* (Paris: Fayard, 1976).

*At the Summit Conference held in Rambouillet (near Paris), November 15-17, 1975.

18. In an article published in *Le Monde* of June 17, 1975, Jacques Rueff wrote: "The crisis ravaging the West appears to all those affected by it as an intolerable scandal."

2

THE LARGE DROP IN PRODUCTION
AND NATIONAL INCOME

Before we consider the steps that should be taken so the world economy can emerge from the present impasse, it is important to examine the nature and effects of this crisis, which began toward the middle of 1973. Today the crisis continues despite the fact that certain—but precarious—encouraging signs of improvement have appeared.[1]

Let us first see how national income has evolved, as indicated by the most recent statistical data. The total production of goods and services (or GNP) in the industrialized countries increased at an average annual rate of 4.8 percent (at constant prices) during 1960–70. But in 1974 GNP declined for the first time since the war, by 0.2 percent. In 1975 the situation worsened and GNP declined by 2 percent as compared with 1974 for the OECD member countries as a whole. The drop in industrial production was even sharper. This recession has been the deepest and longest since

---

1. William Bundy, *The World Economic Crisis* (New York: Norton, 1976).

FIGURE 2.1

Industrial Production in OECD Countries, 1960–75

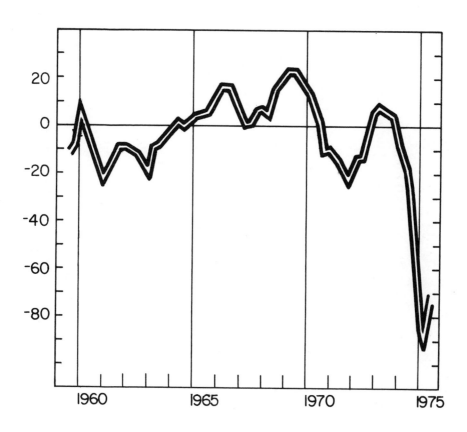

Source: The Economist (London), January 1, 1977.

TABLE 2.1

Growth of GNP in OECD Countries
(percentage changes on an annual basis, adjusted for seasonal variations)

	Average 1963-64 to 1973-74	Change from Previous Year			
		1974	1975	1976	1977[a]
Canada	5.40	3.20	0.60	4.75	3.50
United States	4.00	-1.80	-1.80	6.25	4.50
Japan	9.40	-1.30	2.10	6.00	6.00
France[b]	5.40	3.90	-1.20	5.00	3.00
West Germany	4.40	0.40	-3.20	5.50	3.50
Italy[b]	4.70	3.40	-3.70	4.50	-0.50
United Kingdom[b]	2.70	-0.10	-1.80	1.00	1.50
Total of the above countries	5.00	-0.30	-1.30	5.50	4.00
Other OECD countries[c]	5.00	3.30	-0.60	2.50	2.75
Total OECD	5.00	0.30	-1.20	5.00	3.75

[a]Estimated.
[b]TGDP.
[c]Austria, Belgium, Denmark, Finland, Greece, Ireland, Netherlands, Norway, Spain, Sweden, Switzerland.
Source: Perspectives economiques de l'OCDE, no. 20 (December 1976).

1945. Figure 2.1 shows the evolution of industrial production in the OECD countries during the four great recessions of the postwar period.

GNP data for 1976 indicate that the economies of the industrialized countries were beginning to recover slowly and that the situation was more favorable than for the preceding years (see Table 2.1).

The United States led the way to this higher recovery rate, with a 1976 growth rate of close to 6.25 percent. However, unemployment remained high, at 7.5 percent of the active population, and it appeared likely to remain high for a long time. For this reason, certain experts foresee a slowdown in the growth rate of the American economy in coming years. For Germany and Japan, the forecasts are more optimistic. The 1976 growth rates were 5.5 percent for Germany and 6 percent for Japan. In France, despite a slight economic recovery, the situation remained precarious because of high inflation. However, GNP growth rate was 5 percent for the year 1976.

In the United Kingdom and Italy, the recession continues and it does not appear likely that these countries can very rapidly overcome their difficulties.

For all the OECD countries taken together, GNP will increase by about 3.75 percent during the period until the end of 1977, according to the OECD publication *Perspectives economiques* of December 1976. In other words, a reduced growth rate is to be noted, and this would seem to justify concern about the world economy.

The OECD has tried to bring together the macroeconomic projections of member countries regarding the real and potential evolution of production to 1980. Table 2.2 shows that most countries foresee a slowing down in the growth of total production.

According to the OECD study, this slowdown in growth will reflect two factors: (1) a temporary lack of adaptation between capital and the work force, which will prevent full employment of the active population and (2) a slower increase in labor productivity for a given level of capital accumulation.

However, as mentioned, these forecasts depend on many imponderable factors. The most troublesome are the rates of inflation and unemployment, which will probably be higher than in the 1960s. Therefore, the forecasts simply constitute a possible scenario

TABLE 2.2

Growth of Total Production
(average annual changes, in percentages; GNP or GDP at constant prices)

Country	From Middle to End of the 1960s	Beginning of the 1970s	1974 to 1975	1975 to 1980
United States	3.9	3.5	-2.00	6.25
West Germany	4.4	4.3	-3.75	4.50
France	5.8	5.2	-2.50	5.75
Canada	5.1	5.4	-0.75	5.00
Austria	4.7	5.5	-3.00	3.75
Belgium	4.6	5.0	-2.50	4.25
Finland	5.2	5.0	-1.00	4.75
Sweden	3.7	3.5	0.50	3.75

of future economic development. We must not overlook the fact that forecasts are always hazardous and that specialized research institutes do not always agree. International business cycle repercussions of all kinds may well compromise the accuracy of forecasts.[2]

In the United States, for example, a group of 100 multinational companies use the forecasting services of two of the best known specialized institutions, Data Resources, Inc., and Chase Econometrics Associates, Inc. Forecasts by these institutions published in *Business Week* on April 26, 1976, for the year 1976 demonstrate how difficult is the technique of econometric modeling because of endogenous and exogenous factors and variables.

---

2. These difficulties are analyzed in an article published in the OECD *Observer*, January-February 1976.

TABLE 2.3

GNP Per Capita, 1970 and 1980

Country Grouping	Population 1975 (millions)	Per Capita GNP (dollars)		Annual Growth Rate (percent)
		1970	1980	
Low-income countries (less than $200 per capita per year)	1,000	105	108	0.2
Middle-income countries (more than $200 per capita per year)	715	410	540	2.8
OECD countries	675	3,100	4,000	2.6

Source: Speech by World Bank President Robert McNamara to the Board of Governors, September 1, 1975.

However, these forecasts provide valuable indications for the determination of long-term policies.

In the countries of the Third World between 1960 and 1970 GNP increased at an average annual rate of 5.6 percent. However, the economic situation in the less developed countries remained disturbing during 1975. In fact, the drop of demand in the industrialized countries, the deterioration of the terms of trade of the developing countries, the problems raised for their balances of international payments, and their application of anti-inflationary measures can be considered as brakes on their GNP growth. On the other hand, it must not be forgotten that economic recovery will be slower in these countries because of their chronic problems. According to forecasts by the World Bank, the increase in per capita income in the poorest countries will not be greater than 0.2 percent annually during 1970–80 (see Table 2.3).

The picture given by these forecasts is very disturbing. A billion people, whose per capita income in 1970 was one-thirtieth the per capita income in the industrialized countries, will only have one-fortieth in 1980. For the whole of the decade, the per capita increase in the poor countries will only be $3, whereas in the developed countries this increase will be $900, that is, 300 times greater. In other words, at the end of the decade, a larger and more alarming gap will exist between the rich countries and the poor countries, and a third of the world's population will continue to live in absolute poverty.

HIGH INFLATION

One of the main features of the current world recession is the inflationary flare-up, the most powerful since the war. However, it must be recognized that certain inflationary tendencies also appeared during the 1960–70 decade. Between 1960 and 1972 the index of consumer prices in the industrialized countries increased by more than 50 percent.[3] But especially since 1973 inflationary tendencies have begun to take on disturbing dimensions, reaching unusually high levels in 1974.

The increase in the price of oil made 1974 the international year of excessive and persistent inflation, even though this increase was not the main cause of inflation, as we saw in the preceding chapter. Other factors certainly influenced prices as well. Among these were especially:

1. The large and simultaneous economic growth in the OECD member countries during 1972 and 1973, which led to a streng-

---

3. Between 1960 and 1972, consumer price indexes in certain countries increased as follows (percentages):

Switzerland	58.2
West Germany	45.9
France	67.9
United Kingdom	75.1
Italy	63.1
Japan	97.3
United States	41.7

Source: Union des Banques Suisses, Inflation (Geneva, 1973).

thening of global demand and a ballooning of investments—a large part of which were unproductive.[4]

2. The unprecedented price increases for many primary products.

3. The importation by many countries of inflationary pressures transmitted through the channels of international trade—pressures subsequently reflected in domestic production costs.

4. The behavior of demand which, beginning in 1974 under the pressure of inflation, ultimately accelerated the effects of inflation.

As is indicated by the statistical analyses of the IMF, the average rise in prices in the industrialized countries (adjusted on the basis of the general GNP index) reached 4.8 percent in 1972, 7.0 percent in 1973, and 11.7 percent in 1974—as compared with 3.4 percent for 1960–70.

Even if the variations in the currency reevaluation rates of some countries (in 1974: Japan 24.5 percent, West Germany 7.3 percent) are taken into account, it is undeniable that this inflation has been the strongest during the postwar period (see Tables 2.4 and 2.5).

On the other hand, it should be noted that the strongest inflationary tendencies have occurred in the developing countries. In 1973 the average annual rate of price increases in these countries was double that in the industrialized countries, and in 1974 it reached 16.5 percent. For several countries it went beyond 30 percent.

According to the vice president of the Commission of the European Communities, Wilhelm Haferkamp, the most disturbing

---

4. The *Annual Report* of the International Monetary Fund for 1975, analyzing the causes of inflation and recession, emphasizes the exceptional concurrence of economic expansion in many countries in 1972 and 1973 and points out that the soaring of global demand was due to a certain extent to errors of judgment in the application of monetary and budgetary policies, which turned out to be too expansionist from the viewpoint of the fight against inflation (see IMF *Bulletin*, September 1, 1975). On the problem of inflation, see also: A Meister, *L'Inflation créatrice* (Paris: PUF, 1975); Pierre de Calan, *Chère Inflation* (Paris: Editions France-Empire, 1975).

TABLE 2.4

**Consumers' Prices in Seven Large Countries, 1974–77
(percentage changes as compared with preceding
year, adjusted for seasonal variations)**

Country	1974	1975	1976	1977
Canada	10.6	10.3	7.50	6.50
United States	11.5	8.0	5.00	5.25
Japan	24.5	11.9	9.50	9.50
West Germany	7.3	6.1	4.75	4.00
Italy	19.1	17.0	17.00	20.50
United Kingdom	15.6	23.2	15.00	13.00
France	3.7	11.7	9.50	8.75
Total	13.2	10.3	7.50	7.50

Source: OECD, *Perspectives économiques* (Paris), December 1976.

TABLE 2.5

**Price Increases in the Less Developed Countries
(percentage changes in consumers' prices)**

	Annual Average	Changes in Comparison with Preceding Year		
	1965–70	1972	1973	1974
Economically Less Developed Countries	13	12	21	29
of Africa	6	5	9	17
of Asia	16	8	18	31
of the Middle East	4	6	10	17
of the Western Hemisphere	15	20	29	36

Source: IMF, *Annual Report*, 1975.

fact is that the rise in consumers' prices again began to accelerate in most European countries after 1975—a development that is incompatible with the recovery of economic activity and brings with it the danger of economic collapse when the next crisis comes.[5] Calculated on an annual basis, consumers' prices for the community as a whole increased by an average 11.5 percent during the first ten months of 1976 as compared with 9 percent during the second half of 1975.

A certain general improvement appeared in 1975 and 1976. According to OECD data, the average annual consumers' price increase for member countries was 11.2 percent for 1975, although in the European member states it reached a higher level estimated at 13 percent.

As for the year 1976, the average inflation rate was 8.4 percent, but the risk of a new inflationary impulse was not excluded. Indeed, the inflationary danger continued to be a serious preoccupation for the industrialized countries.

The partial statistical data available on price indexes in the less developed countries also indicate a tendency in 1975 toward a slowing down, except for some isolated cases. The average rate of annual increase for all these countries reached 25 percent.

For certain countries like Argentina, Brazil, Chile, Ghana, Nigeria, Uruguay, and Zaire price increases have been higher than 30 percent.

At this point we want to emphasize not only the impact of worldwide inflation in reducing the real incomes of the developing countries but also the fact that inflation affects operations undertaken to finance the development of these countries. According to World Bank estimates, in 1980 some $3 of financing assistance will be needed to accomplish what could be done in 1965 with $1, and more than $2 will be needed in 1980 to reach the same result as could be attained in 1970 with $1.[6] To make up part of this difference and render it easier for the developing countries to meet in-

---

5. See his statement at the Tripartite Meeting in Luxembourg on June 24, 1976.
6. See Robert McNamara, address to the Board of Governors of the World Bank, September 1, 1975 (Washington, D.C.), p. 6.

creased debt-servicing burdens, the World Bank has decided to create a new financing mechanism called the "third window." But this third window, an emergency measure, has not yet given satisfactory results.

Thus, the problem of inflation has become a worldwide problem affecting all countries, while measures to combat it have all proved ineffective.

GROWING AND DANGEROUSLY HIGH UNEMPLOYMENT

The most painful consequence of the recession is the deterioration in employment. The number of unemployed in the industrialized countries (18 countries of Europe, the United States, Canada, Japan, Australia, and New Zealand) exceeded 17 million in September 1975.[7] This figure, which represents 5.2 percent of the able population, was an increase of 6 million above September 1974. According to the ILO this one-year increase, as well as the total number of unemployed, was the highest in 40 years. Only during the crisis of 1932–34 did the number of unemployed in these countries exceed 25 million.

However, if account is taken of the average number of family members dependent on each worker in the industrialized countries, the total number of unemployed and dependents is 40.4 million, according to the International Labour Office (ILO) estimates. This represents an increase of 14 million in a single year. Table 2.6 shows the distribution of unemployment in the industrialized countries by geographic region and the changes registered in one year.

Although Europe's unemployment rate is lower than the average in the 23 industrialized countries, Europe had more than half of the 6 million additional unemployed registered during 1975. The greatest increases in unemployment took place in Denmark, West Germany, and France.

ILO data show the increase was greater than 50 percent in some 12 countries including particularly Belgium, Spain, Portugal,

---

7. According to ILO estimates (Press Bulletin of November 18, 1975).

TABLE 2.6

Unemployment in September 1975:
ILO Estimates

	Estimated Number of Unemployed (millions)		Average Rate of Unemployment, September 1975 (percentage of the working population)
	September 1975	Increase Since September 1974	
Asia and Oceania (Australia, Japan, and New Zealand)	1.3	+0.4	2.0
Northern Europe (Denmark, Finland, Ireland, Norway, United Kingdom, and Sweden)	2.1	+0.9	5.7
Western Europe (West Germany, Austria, Belgium, France, Netherlands, and Switzerland)	2.9	+1.1	4.4
Southern Europe (Spain, Greece, Italy, Portugal, Turkey, and Yugoslavia)	2.7	+1.0	4.0
North America (Canada and the United States)	8.1	+2.5	8.1
Total	17.1	+5.9	5.2

Source: ILO, *World Employment Program,* Report on the World of Labour and Development (Geneva, 1975).

25

and the United Kingdom.[8] In the United Kingdom, in July 1975, the total number of unemployed exceeded 1 million for the first time since April 1940. In France the number of unsatisfied demands for employment also was more than 1 million in October and November 1975. In West Germany, for the first time in more than 20 years, the number of unemployed was higher than 1 million from January 1975 through December of that year (1,223,000 unemployed were registered in December as compared with 946,000 in December 1974 and 486,000 in December 1973).

The increase of unemployment in 1975 is even more striking if account is taken of two phenomena: that the average duration of unemployment appears to have lengthened while partial unemployment appears to have increased considerably in many industrialized countries. This employment crisis provides a basis for the forecast that unemployment will remain high in 1977 in North America and Japan. This also is likely in certain European countries.

In the United States unemployment increased greatly during 1975. In March 1975 there were 8,300,000 persons without employment or about 3,300,000 more than in March 1974, and the proportion of unemployed to the total working population reached 8.1 percent—the highest rate since 1941. However, between March and December 1975 some 1,100,000 workers were able to find jobs and the unemployment rate dropped slightly below the level of 7.2 percent.

Although some governments took defensive measures aimed at reducing average working time or the supply of manpower to improve conditions on the labor market, unemployment has remained high and will remain high for a considerable time.

This employment crisis has been felt particularly by the young and by women. In the industrialized countries almost 50 percent of the unemployed are between 15 and 25 years of age (see Table 2.7). In France 46 percent of the unemployed in October 1975 were under 25 years old, and some 450,000 out of 700,000 unemployed were looking for their first jobs.

---

8. ILO, *World Employment Programme, 1975*, Report on the World of Labour and Development (Geneva, February 1976), p. 39.

TABLE 2.7

Distribution of Unemployment by Age Groups, 1975
(percentages)

Country	Unemploy-ment as a Percentage of the Work-ing Popu-lation	By Age Groups		
		15–24	25–54	55 and over
Australia	4.2	55	39	6
Canada	7.0	49	43	8
France	4.1	46	49	5
West Germany	4.4	28	60	12
Italy	3.6	64	34	2
Japan	1.9	23	59	18
Sweden	2.7	37	42	21
United Kingdom	3.2	42	41	17
United States	8.3	46	46	8

Source: "Perspectives économiques de l'OECD," *OECD Economic Outlook* (December 20, 1976).

According to an OECD study, the young now appear for the first time as a disfavored category in the employment picture, together with immigrants, women, aged workers, and ethnic minorities.[9] This problem is a major preoccupation for many governments because the difficulties faced by young people in entering active economic life are not merely cyclical but also structural, and a new policy both short and long term is required. If the present situation continues, there is a risk that great social tensions will be unleashed.

---

9. See OECD *Observer*, no. 77 (September-October 1975).

The situation in the developing countries is even more dramatic. Although the available information on unemployment in these countries is incomplete, it is estimated that in 1970—when economic conditions were normal—the number of unemployed might have been between 76 and 122 million. But, as stated in another ILO study, "the statistics on declared unemployment cannot give any realistic idea of the general poverty which exists."[10]

In these countries seasonal unemployment is widespread and underemployment is a prevailing condition. But "the most widespread and most critical phenomenon is quite simply that work gives poor workers an income which is insufficient to satisfy their essential needs."

It is estimated that the number of poor in the developing market-type economies—that is, not including the Communist countries—amounts to some 1,200 million of whom about 700 million live in the most complete misery.

What is most disturbing is that in coming years, due to an accelerated increase in the number of workers and the demographic explosion, pressures are likely to increase the number of unemployed to between 400 and 500 million by 1980. In addition, according to United Nations calculations, the labor supply of all the developing countries taken together (China included) may be expected to increase by some 75 percent between 1975 and 2000, when it will reach almost 2 billion. This new situation, whose dimensions are part of the unknown, will arise to further complicate the problem of economic development in the less developed countries.[11]

Thus, as a result of present developments, governments are not faced with the choice between inflation and unemployment as they were in the early postwar period. Today governments must deal with a more terrifying problem: the coexistence of inflation and unemployment or what is termed "stagflation."

The present situation, which has overturned the classic theory of the relationship between inflation and unemployment, is made

---

10. ILO, *L'Emploi, la croissance et les besoins essentielles: Problème mondial* (Geneva, 1976), p. 17.
11. ILO, *World Employment Program* (Geneva, 1976).

more difficult by the fact that the labor market no longer functions normally. Policies directed against unemployment do not succeed in resolving the problem of full employment. Furthermore, the functioning of the labor market deteriorates even more because social policies—applied because unemployment is so extensive—create new bottlenecks that prevent labor mobility and add supplementary inflationary pressures.[12]

Indeed, this disturbing situation, which predominates in the world labor market, not only has social effects but also serious economic effects. Among the latter should be particularly emphasized those related to unemployment benefits paid by the state, especially in the industrialized countries. According to an OECD study, this financial aid to the unemployed amounts in some cases to 2 percent of the national income. In Canada, West Germany, and Japan unemployment benefits vary from 60 to 80 percent of former wages. In the United States jobless aid increased from $4.1 billion in 1972 to more than $17 billion in 1975.

Thus, at a a time when world production is stagnating or declining, a constantly increasing portion of the world's wealth, which during 1960–70 was devoted to the output of productive goods and services, is now used to ensure unemployment benefits—which are socially indispensable, but intensify inflationary pressures on a worldwide scale. We shall return to this problem in a later chapter when we examine the Keynesian theory of full employment.

If it is accepted that the sums devoted to unemployment insurance by Western industrial countries amount to $25 billion for the 17 million unemployed,[13] it would appear that by using

---

12. A very clear analysis of the relations between unemployment and inflation, with an interpretation of the theory of the British economist A. W. Phillips, has been presented by Philippe Simonnot in his book *L'Avenir du système monétaire* (Paris: R. Laffont, 1972), pp. 56 ff.

13. The United States with 8 million unemployed spends $17 billion annually for unemployment payments.

these funds for productive investments a supplementary output of $33 billion could be obtained.[14]

---

14. We have made this estimate using calculations similar to those of OECD. Based on data for five European countries, an investment of one dollar brings about an additional output of 30 cents. The ratio is higher for Japan and for the developing countries. See OECD, *La Croissance de la production, 1960–1970* (Paris, December 1970), p. 295.

3

INTERNATIONAL TRADE AND
BALANCE-OF-PAYMENTS
DEFICITS

THE LARGE DEFICITS OF
THE OIL-CONSUMING COUNTRIES

After inflation and unemployment, the third serious problem facing the international economy arises from the deterioration of payments balances, and particularly from the large deficits in the current accounts of countries that are not oil producers. This situation results from a general modification in the structure of international trade and monetary transfer, which has led to surpluses in the current accounts of the oil-producing countries.

The recession has directly influenced the evolution of international trade. World trade—after rising (by volume) less rapidly in 1974 than in preceding years—sharply declined in 1975. This unfavorable change first appeared in the industrialized countries and subsequently was extended to the raw materials-producing countries (except the oil-producing countries).

The slowdown in the growth of trade was accompanied by a deceleration in the increase of prices for exported products. But this did not occur at either the same rate or the same time in all countries. The central element in these price fluctuations was the increase in oil prices, which constituted the activating force behind

TABLE 3.1

Current Accounts Balances
(in billions of dollars)

Country	1974	1975	1976	1977
Canada	−1.7	−4.9	−4.0	−3.5
United States	−0.6	+11.7	−1.3	−3.0
Japan	−4.7	−0.7	+3.8	0.0
France	−6.0	−0.1	−6.0	−3.8
West Germany	+9.7	+3.9	+4.0	+5.0
Italy	−8.0	−0.6	−2.8	−0.5
Netherlands	−2.0	+1.6	+2.0	+2.8
United Kingdom	−8.7	−3.7	−3.3	−1.3
Belgium	+0.6	+0.3	−0.3	−0.3
Greece	−1.2	−1.0	−0.9	−1.0
Other countries	−14.4	−13.0	−13.7	−12.9
Total OECD	−33.0	−6.5	−22.5	−17.5

Source: OECD, *Economic Outlook*, December 20, 1976.

the upset in payments balances. But other factors also must be borne in mind. For the upset was sparked by the widespread practice of exchange rate fluctuations, introduced after the first quarter of 1973 by countries with strong currencies, and by the fact that economic activity reached a point of culmination in the industrialized countries.

In 1975, for the first time since World War II, the volume of world trade showed a decline—of about 6 percent.

The changes in payments balances differed not only from country to country but also for groups of countries—industrialized, developing, OPEC, and non-OPEC countries including the socialist countries. Table 3.1 shows the evolution of the current payments balances of some industrialized countries during the years 1974, 1975, and 1976, and the perspectives for 1977.

The most striking aspect of this evolution was the spectacular reduction in the deficit of the industrialized countries: from $33 billion for 1974 to $6.5 billion in 1975. For 1976 the deficit was $22.5 billion, while for 1977 a deficit of about $17.1 billion is foreseen.[1]

The reduction in the global payments deficit of the OECD countries as compared with 1974 may be explained by the improvement in the large industrial countries, especially the United States and Germany. About two-thirds of the improvement in the commercial balance, and consequently in the balance of payments of the OECD countries, is imputable to their exports to the OPEC countries. As regards the volume of the deficit in 1976 for all OECD countries together, it was determined in part by changes in the current balances of the United States, Japan, and France.

On the other hand, the deficit in the current accounts of the small OECD countries remained at the level of $13 billion in 1975 and 1976, a deficit almost equal to that of 1974. The same deficit may probably continue during 1977.

In developing countries that are not oil producers, the current accounts deficit increased in 1975 to $32.5 billion. It was $24 billion in 1976. For 1977 a deficit of about $26.5 billion is foreseen (see Table 3.2).

A large number of these countries have been obliged to pay much higher prices not only for their oil imports but also for imported food products, fertilizers, and other goods without being able to compensate for part of these losses by increasing their exports to the OPEC countries.

In the "other countries" group, including the Sino-Soviet area, South Africa, Israel, and Yugoslavia, the deficit was $4 billion in 1973 and reached $6.5 billion in 1974, $14 billion for 1975 and $12.5 billion in 1976.

FINANCING THE DEFICITS

Overcoming the foreign exchange deficit created by the increase in oil prices clearly has been a preoccupation for the consuming

---

1. See OECD, *Economic Outlook*, no. 20 (December 1976).

TABLE 3.2
Current Accounts Balances, by Group
(in billions of dollars)

Current Accounts Balance (including official transfers)	1973	1974	1975	1976	1977[b]
OECD	2.5	-33.0	-6.5	-22.5	-17.5
OPEC	3.5	65.5	34.5	42.0	36.5
Developing countries (non-oil producers)	-2.5	-21.5	-32.5	-24.0	-26.5
Others[a]	-4.0	-6.5	-14.0	-12.5	-14.5
Errors and omissions	-0.5	4.5	-18.0	-17.0	-22.0

[a]Sino-Soviet region, South Africa, Israel, Cyprus, Malta, and Yugoslavia.
[b]Estimated.
Source: OECD, *Perspectives économiques*, no. 21 (December 1976).

countries. However, the problem was less severe for the industrialized countries because their payments balances were strengthened through the recycling of petrodollars and increased imports by the oil-producing countries.

The countries producing basic materials (not including oil), unlike the industrialized countries, benefited more modestly from petrodollars accorded as loans or direct gifts, but these covered only a small part of their current accounts deficits. Therefore, they were obliged to have recourse to complementary sources of financing, in particular through the capital markets of the industrialized countries, the IMF, and other international bodies.

In fact, to cover the balance-of-payments deficits use is made of funds supplied on a massive scale as credits and international financial transfers. The greatest portion of such funds comes from the OPEC countries, which export a large volume of capital. This financing has taken several forms: foreign exchange loans contracted by the central authorities or by state-control led enterprises of the

FIGURE 3.1

New Issues of Eurobonds
(in millions of dollars)

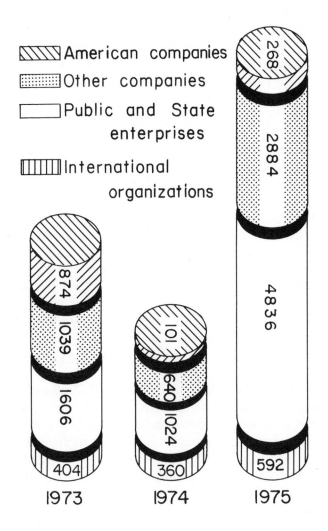

American companies
Other companies
Public and State enterprises
International organizations

268
2884
4836
592
1975

874
1039
1606
404
1973

101
640
1024
360
1974

Source: Morgan Guaranty Trust Co.

borrowing countries; investment of a large volume of oil funds in the money markets; and financing through American and European banks.

All these operations between creditors and borrowers, conducted through banks and official institutions, played a particularly important role in covering the deficits of 1974, which were on the order of $33 billion. According to the Morgan Guaranty Trust Co., new international bond issues totaled $19.9 billion in 1975 as compared with $6.9 billion in 1974 and $7.8 billion in 1973.[2] It should be noted that $15.2 billion of the new 1975 issues were taken by the industrialized countries, while the developing countries only obtained $800 million, or the same amount as in 1973 (see Figure 3.1).

According to OECD statistics, the portion of the long-term debt of the developing countries that is linked to financing current accounts deficits amounted to an estimated $16.2 billion for 1973 and $22.6 billion in 1975. Since this deficit will certainly continue at a high level during the coming years, it follows that previous obligations in the form of loans for development will be compounded by new indebtedness not linked to productive investments.

Table 3.3 clearly indicates the evolution of the current accounts deficits and the total indebtedness of the developing countries, as well as the sources of financing. However, some differences may be noted between Tables 3.2 and 3.3 with respect to the estimated deficits for 1975 and 1976. These differences are certainly due to adjustment factors such as reduction in exports and cost of oil.

To cover deficits in their payments balances, all countries have had to borrow, especially in 1974. As a result, they now are confronted with serious overindebtedness. This is of particular gravity for the developing countries, as we shall see in more detail in a later chapter. Table 3.3 indicates that amortization of the foreign debt of the developing countries required $9 billion in 1974, $10 billion in 1975, and $11.5 billion in 1976. The situation is even worse for the poorest countries.

Limits on indebtedness also exist for the industrialized countries which have had recourse to borrowing to meet the large

---

2. See *World Financial Markets*, December 1976.

TABLE 3.3

Financing of Developing Countries Outside OPEC
(in billions of dollars)

	1973	1974	Esti- mated 1975	Pro- jected 1976
Financing requirements (gross)				
Current accounts*	−9.0	−26.0	−34.0	−29.0
Amortization of				
foreign debt	−8.5	−9.0	−10.0	−11.5
Total requirements	−17.5	−35.0	−44.0	−40.5
Financing sources (gross)				
Official	15.1	−	−	−
Changes in reserves at				
official exchange rates	−8.3	−2.8	2.5	2.5
Direct private invest-				
ments (net)	3.6	3.6	3.5	3.5
Commercial credits	10.3	16.5	19.5	12.0
Others	−3.2	−3.5	−6.25	−5.5

*Not including official transfers.

Source: Morgan Guaranty Trust Co., *World Financial Markets*, (Paris), January 21, 1976.

deficits incurred during 1974 (see Table 3.4). Public sector borrowing in the United States was in the order of $6.5 billion in 1974 and $7.0 billion in 1975; in Germany it was DM 24 billion in 1974 and DM 67 billion in 1975. The problem was similar in the United Kingdom, which had recourse to increases in the public debt on the order of $36 billion in 1973 and $52 billion in 1974.[3] The external debt of the United States, both short- and long-term, rose from $47 billion at the end of 1970 to $126 billion at the end of 1975.

---

3. See OECD, *Perspectives économiques*, no. 17 (Paris, July 1975): 50.

TABLE 3.4

National Indebtedness, 1975

Country	Increased Indebtedness as a Percent of GNP	Debt Servicing as a Percent of Taxes Collected	Debts Out-standing as a Percent of GNP
United Kingdom	12.1	13.5	80
Italy	9.8	12.6	48
West Germany	7.3	6.9	25
Austria	5.7	5.3	21
Switzerland	5.4	5.2	24
Japan	5.3	9.3	14
Belgium	4.8	–	48
United States	4.7	–	51
Sweden	4.4	5.6	39
France	3.1	3.7	12

Source: See OECD, *Perspectives économiques*, no. 17 (Paris, July 1975), p. 50.

The financing of all countries—both industrialized and developing—through the Euromarket has taken on disturbing dimensions and poses problems for international monetary authorities. Eurobank credits totaled $197 billion at the end of 1975. These loans represented the counterpart of deposits resulting from the increased reserves of countries other than the United States (the OPEC countries) or from the liquid funds of commercial banks and individuals in these countries.

The fact that each deficit country is in a position to obtain a loan on the international money market increases the world's foreign exchange reserves and thus can lead to additional inflationary effects. In fact, since 1973 the Euromarket has become the primary source of international liquidity. This situation disturbs the Central Bank of West Germany, which in its 1975 annual report emphasizes that this system "can lead to a dangerous accumulation of foreign exchange indebtedness." The Bundesbank added in this report:

> Nor can it be overlooked that the rapid growth in the world's foreign exchange reserves during the six years from 1970 to 1975 representing a total of $149 billion, or 190 percent, has given a powerful impetus to international liquidity and that this can bring about a large inflationary effect in the future.[4]

Subsequently the Bundesbank criticized the International Monetary Fund for having acted too much like an institution for foreign exchange assistance, resulting in the creation of an international financial market that tries to deal with the payments deficits of various countries without posing economic conditions—and very often without an overall view of the borrowing country's indebtedness. This leads to deterioration in the quality of loans; thus, loans should be coordinated and controlled by the IMF to avoid unfavorable repercussions on economic policy.

Thus, as Guido Carli, former governor of the Bank of Italy, has written, "at the present time there is no world monetary system capable of giving the system of international payments the necessary liquidity which would permit a further expansion of world trade."[5] Even worse, the control of international liquidity—which should be the responsibility of the IMF—is actually exercised by private banks, particularly the American banks. This means that in times of difficulty everything will depend on the attitude of the Federal Reserve Board, and in the final analysis on the U.S. Congress. Are we aware of this danger? Let us not forget that the major part of the $150 billion increase in international monetary reserves between 1970 and 1975 was made up of official dollar claims against the United States. This shows the complete disorder reigning in the present international monetary system. It carries the risk of a permanent monetary crisis.[6]

---

4. A summary of this report was published in the *International Herald Tribune* (Paris), April 30, 1976.

5. See IMF, *Bulletin*, July 26, 1976.

6. M. Brennan, *The Politics of International Monetary Reform* (Cambridge, Mass.: Ballinger, 1976).

4

THE INCOME OF
THE OIL-PRODUCING
COUNTRIES

MOVEMENT OF CAPITAL TOWARD
THE OPEC COUNTRIES

The multiplication of the oil price has created, as we have seen, an unprecedented shift of capital from the oil-consuming countries toward the oil-producing countries. The effect has been the accumulation of enormous monetary surpluses in the oil-producing countries.[1]

In fact, while in 1973 the total payments received by the OPEC countries for their oil exports did not exceed $25 billion, in 1974 such payments amounted to $95 billion and in 1975 to $98 billion. According to later revised estimates (January 1976), the export receipts of the OPEC countries, including receipts for exports other than oil, might have been $113 billion in 1975.

This unprecedented increase in the receipts of the OPEC countries has led to an expansion of their imports from an average annual rate of less than 4.5 percent in 1960–70 to a rate of about 37 percent in 1974. Most of these imports, it should be noted,

---

1. A. Rustow and J. Mugno, *OPEC Success and Prospects* (New York: Council on Foreign Relations Books, 1976).

TABLE 4.1

Surpluses of the OPEC Countries on Their Oil Accounts
(in billions of dollars)

	1973			1974			1975		
	Oil Income	Import	Surplus	Oil Income	Import	Surplus	Oil Income	Import	Surplus
Algeria	1.0	-2.1	-0.9	3.7	-3.7	0.4	3.6	-5.7	-2.0
Ecuador	0.1	-0.5	-0.1	0.5	-0.8	0.1	0.4	-0.9	-0.1
Indonesia	1.2	-2.4	-0.4	3.4	-3.9	0.2	3.7	-4.7	-0.3
Iran	4.5	-3.6	1.1	18.7	-8.0	10.7	19.9	-10.6	9.6
Iraq	1.7	-1.2	0.5	5.7	-3.5	2.0	7.6	-6.6	0.5
Kuwait	1.9	-0.9	1.5	8.0	-1.5	7.3	7.9	-2.1	7.1
Libya	2.3	-2.2	-0.6	6.2	-3.0	2.5	5.2	-4.1	0.6
Nigeria	2.4	-1.8	0.3	7.6	-2.5	5.2	6.7	-5.1	1.9
Qatar	0.4	-0.2	0.1	1.6	-0.3	1.3	1.8	-0.4	1.3
Saudi Arabia	5.5	-1.8	3.1	24.6	-3.5	20.8	26.7	-5.7	20.1
United Arab Emirates	1.2	-0.9	0.3	6.0	-1.6	4.4	6.5	-2.2	4.2
Venezuela	3.0	-2.8	-0.1	8.9	-4.7	4.0	8.3	-6.5	1.8
Total	25.2	-20.4	4.8	94.9	-37.0	58.9	98.3	-54.6	44.7

Note: Imports are f.o.b. The surplus is calculated after deduction of nonpetroleum exports, payments for services, and private transfers.

Source: U.S. Treasury Department.

came from the industrialized countries, which supplied the OPEC countries with manufactured products, capital and consumer goods, technology, and especially arms.

If we deduct from the receipts of the OPEC countries the cost of their imports, they have benefited from a monetary (or petro-dollar) surplus estimated at $4.8 billion in 1973, $58.5 billion in 1974, and $44.7 billion in 1975. Table 4.1 reflects the situation in the oil-producing countries between 1973 and 1975, although for statistical reasons figures given are slightly different from the OECD estimates.

As a result of this movement of capital, the world economy will experience profound upheavals during the next 25 years.[2] The first consequence of this tremendous transfer of wealth to the oil-producing countries, whose population does not exceed 300 million, is a rapid and permanent increase in their per capita GNP. Kuwait in 1975 had the highest per capita GNP in the world: $11,365 as compared with $7,020 for the United States.[3]

Available data indicate that beginning in 1975 conditions changed in a very striking manner but without reversing the trend. The oil-consuming countries undergoing a generalized recession made efforts to limit the deficits in their payments balances, and the recession also led to a slowing of the rate of increase of petroleum demand. This made it necessary for certain oil-producing countries to reduce output. (See Table 4.2 and Figure 4.1.) Thus, they suffered the reverse shockwaves of the recession, and this particularly affected countries with limited financial resources. Once again the high degree of interdependence among national economies was demonstrated.

The estimates for 1975, which showed a decline in production of 13.6 percent as compared with 1974, are confirmed by data on the volume of 1975 exports. According to an announcement on April 20, 1976, by the Ministry of Mines and Hydrocarbons of Venezuela, the worldwide exports of oil from the OPEC countries dropped by 12.4 percent in 1975. They reached a daily average in

---

2. See also the book by Philippe Heymann and B. Berteloot, *Aujourd'hui et demain* (Paris: Faltès, 1974).

3. Union Bank of Switzerland, *Notices économiques*, June 1976.

TABLE 4.2

Oil Production, 1973–75
(millions of barrels a day)

	1973	1974	1975
Iran	5.86	6.06	5.75
Iraq	1.93	1.89	1.75
Saudi Arabia	7.60	8.48	7.30
Kuwait	3.02	2.55	2.00
Abu-Dhabi	1.30	1.42	1.15
Qatar	0.57	0.52	0.45
Oman	0.29	0.29	0.35
Dubai	0.22	0.24	0.30
Bahrein	0.07	0.08a	0.10
Sharjah and U.b	—	0.02	0.07
Subtotal	20.86	21.55	19.22
Algeria	1.10	1.04	1.00
Libya	2.17	1.56	1.25
Subtotal	3.27	2.60	2.25
Nigeria and Gabon	2.21	2.43	2.20
Venezuela-Ecuador	3.58	3.13	2.90
Indonesia	1.34	1.34	1.40
Subtotal	7.13	6.90	6.50
Total	31.26	31.05	27.97

aEstimated.
bUnion of Arab Emirates (the old Trucial States).
Source: John Percival, *Oil Wealth*, 1975.

1975 of only 29,235,000 barrels a day (1,480 million tons for the year) as compared with 33,360,000 barrels in 1974 (1,665 million tons for that year).

It is noteworthy that the Soviet Union in 1975 took third place among the world's oil exporters, thereby displacing Venezuela.

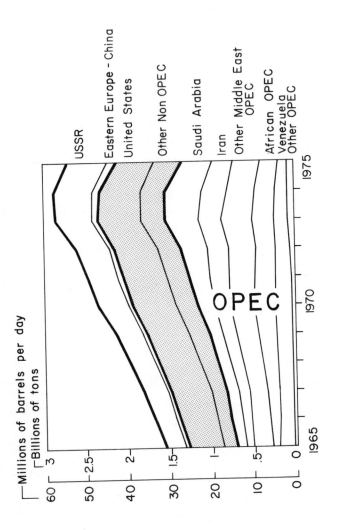

FIGURE 4.1
World Oil Production. 1965-75

Source: BP statistical review of the world oil industry, 1975.

The main exporting countries (in millions of barrels per day) were:

Saudi Arabia	6.90	(7.48 in 1974)
Iran	4.97	(5.76 in 1974)
Venezuela	2.11	(2.75 in 1974)
Kuweit	1.92	(2.39 in 1974)
Nigeria	1.70	(2.18 in 1974)
Indonesia	1.09	(1.16 in 1974)
Soviet Union	2.81	

Had the prospects for a progressive economic recovery been realized in 1976, some changes in the oil markets might have been expected to occur, bringing about an increase in the international trade in oil, although on a limited scale.

According to estimates made by the Morgan Guaranty Trust Co., the global current accounts balance of the OPEC countries for 1974, 1975, and 1976 would evolve as indicated in Table 4.3.

Thus the current accounts surplus of the OPEC countries reached its high point in 1974. In 1975, as in 1976, this surplus was considerably lower.

These estimates differ from those presented in Table 4.1, which were made by the U.S. Treasury; instead of a surplus of $44.7 billion indicated by U.S. authorities for 1975, the Morgan Guaranty Trust Co. foresaw only a $29 billion surplus. On the other hand, the OECD has estimated the surplus in the current accounts balance for

TABLE 4.3

Global Current Accounts Balances of the OPEC Countries (in billions of dollars)

	1974	1975	1976
Income from oil exports	101	100	113
Exports, excluding oil	10	9	10
Imports of goods and services	53	87	104
Income from capital exports	4	7	9
Surplus on current accounts	62	29	28

Source: Morgan Guaranty Trust Co., *World Financial Markets*, January 12, 1976.

1975 at $40 to 50 billion, a figure that conforms to the U.S. Treasury estimate.

The deficit for the OECD member countries, which reached $6.5 billion in 1975, was expected to be $20 billion in 1976 as compared with $33.3 billion in 1974.

Conversely, developments in other countries appeared less satisfactory. The global deficits in their balances on current accounts were higher in 1975 than in 1974, and a significant improvement was foreseen only for 1976.

LONG-TERM PERSPECTIVES FOR OIL SURPLUSES

In the prevailing international trade setting, the crisis tends to be of prolonged duration, especially for the countries producing raw materials (except oil). The effect is to make even more complex the difficult problem of their long-term development. On the other hand, the industrialized countries, having more flexible economic structures, can more easily overcome the cyclical difficulties.

Nevertheless, in the light of new factors in the international economy, it would seem unlikely that the economic recovery in the industrialized countries will run a serene course in 1977, especially with respect to unemployment. And this is all the more true because new developments and factors all over the world are influencing the projected formation of a new international economic and social order, which cannot fail to play a predominant role in shaping the future.

The factors that will determine the evolution of the current accounts balance of the OPEC countries during the coming decade will be oil exports, imports, income from foreign investments, and the financial assistance that these countries furnish to the other developing countries. This evolution will determine the size of the petrodollar surplus.

First, as regards oil exports the estimates are conditional, depending on many factors. The OECD, which revised its previous estimates in January 1976, foresees that the total volume of oil exports could increase on average by 2 to 3 percent a year beginning in 1976 and amount in 1980 to some $130 billion (1975 basis) or

31 to 32 million barrels a day. These exports could subsequently increase somewhat more rapidly to reach about $150 billion in 1985, or 36 to 37 million barrels a day, according to the OECD.

On the other hand, it is necessary to take into account exports of goods other than oil that are expected to show a large increase. Thus, total exports from the OPEC countries might be valued at about $140 billion in 1980 and some $165 to 170 billion in 1985.

However, it must be added that these OECD projections are based on the expectation of a weak demand for oil from the industrialized countries. Between 1976 and 1980 the average increase foreseen is between 4 and 4.5 percent annually. This demand is far below the real long-term production possibilities of the OPEC countries, especially since at present only 72 percent of overall extraction capacity is used.

Another problem will face the OPEC countries when they begin to benefit from their development plans. They will then have a further increase in the volume of their exports, which will bring them additional receipts on foreign exchange accounts.

As noted, the level of the foreign exchange surpluses arising from oil exports will depend on the volume of the imports of the OPEC countries. On this point the various studies and forecasts agree. It may already be foreseen that until 1980 imports will follow a decreasing rhythm while import patterns will show important differences from country to country. These import variations are linked to the oil export market and will be influenced by the absorptive capacity of the OPEC countries. There also will be differences from one country to another as a function of the existing socioeconomic level and the development programs undertaken. On these programs will largely depend the composition of the oil-producing countries' imports of machinery, durable consumer goods, and other products.

The oil-producing countries have already developed ambitious programs to accelerate their development and improve living standards.

OECD makes a distinction between two categories of OPEC countries: (1) those that will probably spend all their export receipts (Algeria, Iran, Iraq, Nigeria, Indonesia, Ecuador, Ven-

ezuela, Gabon) and (2) those whose import demand will remain
lower than their export receipts (Saudi Arabia, Kuweit, the Gulf
States, and Libya).

The government of Saudi Arabia, whose proven oil reserves
are the largest in the world, amounting to more than 100 billion
barrels (7.3 barrels equals 1 ton), intends to use its oil sales receipts in the most effective manner possible. The new five-year
plan that came into operation in 1975–76 foresees total expenditures of about $140 billion. The investments envisaged will be nine
times greater than those of the preceding plan. It is estimated that
realization of the plan should more than double the gross domestic
product (GDP) by 1980.

About $23 billion of the budgetary expenditures envisaged
for the fiscal year 1975–76 are devoted to infrastructure and
industrialization. In order to adapt the infrastructure to the needs
of industrialization, the plan provides that more than 13,000
kilometers of roads will be completed by 1980, that 200,000
dwellings will be constructed, that the supply of electricity to
main cities will be assured, and that port development will be
continued so as to cope better with a continuous increase in mari-
time traffic.

Iran and Iraq, for their part, follow a policy of industrialization designed to reduce their dependence on oil exports.

The OECD countries are the main source of the imports
needed by the OPEC countries for the realization of their development programs. The exports of OECD countries to OPEC
countries have grown from $16.5 billion in 1973 to almost $30
billion in 1974 and about $50 billion in 1975. As a result, the share
of the OPEC countries in the total exports of the industrialized
countries rose from 4 percent to more than 10 percent in 1975.
The largest OECD countries furnish almost 85 percent of the total
exports from the OECD area to the OPEC market (see Table 4.4).

It is difficult to predict the probable import demand of the
OPEC countries over the long term. Much will depend on the
absorptive capacity of each country. According to a study made
by the U.S. Treasury Department, total imports for 1980 and 1985
are estimated at $90 billion and $133 billion. These estimates
represent an annual rate of growth in real terms of 16 percent for

TABLE 4.4

**Recent Development of Exports from OECD Countries
to OPEC Countries, and Market Shares**

	1973		1975 (first half)	
	Share of Exports to OPEC Countries[a]	Market Shares[b]	Share of Exports to OPEC Countries[a]	Market Shares[b]
United States	5.25	22.00	9.50	22.50
Japan	7.50	16.75	15.00	17.50
France	5.00	10.50	8.75	10.50
West Germany	3.25	13.75	7.00	14.00
Italy	5.25	7.50	10.75	7.75
United Kingdom	6.00	11.25	10.75	10.50
Greece	3.25	–	12.75	–
Total OECD	4.25	100.00	8.00	100.00

[a]Percentage of total exports.
[b]Percentage of total OECD countries' exports to OPEC countries.
Source: OECD, *Economic Outlook*, no. 17 (Paris: January 15, 1975).

the period 1975–80 and of about 8 percent for the 1981–85 period, equal to the rate for the 1968–73 period. These estimates are higher in absolute terms than those presented by the OECD, but the rate of growth remains the same (see Table 4.5).

During the period 1980–85, the annual rate of increase in imports for the OPEC countries as a whole will be below 10 percent except for Saudi Arabia, where a rapid acceleration is expected. For Kuweit and the Gulf Emirates, the rate is expected to remain relatively constant. For Iran and Indonesia, a sharp drop in the rate of imports increase must be envisaged.

A country-by-country analysis taking into account present levels of development and different growth factors in each of the

OPEC countries would make possible an identification of the con-
straints affecting real income from oil exports.

It must not be forgotten that the ambition of the OPEC
countries is to be able to carry out accelerated economic development plans and to play an every more important role in international economic and political life. This will depend on many
factors, especially the evolution of the energy problem.

It should, however, be added that the imports of the OPEC
countries will not be supplied entirely by the industrialized countries. To what extent this will be the case will depend on the
possibilities and capacity for substitution of imports from the
recently established industries in the OPEC countries as a group.

TABLE 4.5

Value of Imports by the OPEC Countries
(f.o.b., in billions of U.S. dollars at 1974 prices)

	1974	1980	1985
Algeria	3.7	6.5	10.0
Ecuador	0.8	1.5	2.2
Indonesia	3.9	9.4	12.3
Iran	8.0	24.4	32.0
Iraq	3.5	9.5	14.0
Kuwait	1.5	3.4	6.4
Libya	3.0	5.2	6.5
Nigeria	2.5	8.5	12.6
Qatar	0.3	0.6	0.9
Saudi Arabia	3.5	7.5	17.4
United Arab Emirates	1.6	3.9	6.9
Venezuela	4.7	9.4	12.0
Total	37.0	89.8	133.2
OECD estimate f.o.b.	32.0	78.5	114.0

Source: Gerald Parsky, "The Absorptive Capacity of the OPEC Countries," U.S. Treasury Department, September 5, 1975, p. 6.

TABLE 4.6

Possible Evolution of Current Balances of the OPEC Countries (in billions of 1975 dollars)

	1975	1980	1985
Oil exports, f.o.b.	106.5	129.5	150.0
Other exports, f.o.b.	6.5	10.5	17.0
Imports, f.l.b.	54.5	98.0	145.0
Commercial balance	58.5	42.0	22.0
Services and private transfers	-12.0	-6.5	-13.5
Public transfers	-3.5	-3.5	-3.5
Current balance	43.0	32.0	5.0

Source: OECD, Revised Forecasts, 1980-85, no. 19 (January 1976), and Economic Outlook, no. 18 (December 1975).

Even if this potential capacity is realized and favorable prospects appear for the creation of new trade flows, various circumstances—such as technological difficulties, industrial start-up problems, and the need to train specialized manpower—may delay entrance into certain markets within the OPEC area. But it is nonetheless true that the export potential must be recognized by the industrialized countries.

On the basis of the projections prepared by experts in the United States and OECD, we may estimate the evolution of the current balance of payments of the OPEC countries in 1980 and 1985 (see Table 4.6).

According to the estimates shown in Table 4.6, the current deficit of the OECD countries, which in 1975 was about $43 billion, could fall to some $30 billion in 1980 and be close to zero in 1985. Thus, the total cumulative surplus of the OPEC countries from 1974 to 1980 could be on the order of $250 billion (1975 dollars) and could, on the basis of the OECD projections, reach stability by 1985.

All these projections rest on certain hypotheses, so changes in the assumptions could enormously influence the results. If the relative price of oil increases, the cumulative deficit for the OECD countries will be greater, while the contrary will be true if the pirce is lowered. It has been calculated that a fall of $3 in the relative price could reduce the cumulative deficit by some $80 billion.

THE ROLE OF OIL IN THE ENERGY PROBLEM

The role that the OPEC countries will play on the international economic and political scene will depend on numerous factors, especially the evolution of the energy problem. In effect, the situation created by the quadrupling of oil prices constitutes for the industrialized countries "one of the most important challenges with which they have been confronted in the past twenty five years," as stated in an OECD study on energy.[4]

The OECD study tries to evaluate long-term trends in the energy field. It seeks to answer the question of how the energy needs of the OECD member countries will be met at the beginning of the 1980s if oil prices remain at present levels. The evaluations in the report are based on three hypotheses: (1) the basic hypothesis, which was elaborated in 1973 before the energy crisis; (2) the "$9 per barrel" hypothesis; and (3) the "$6 per barrel" hypothesis.

All these projections are based on forecasts of economic growth prepared before the oil crisis. Undoubtedly, the current slowing down of economic growth will probably have a great influence on energy consumption projections, particularly on oil imports. According to the estimates in the OECD study, the total consumption of energy would increase up to 1985 at an annual rate of 3.54 percent instead of the 5 percent predicted prior to the large increase in the price of oil. Figure 4.2 presents two hypotheses: the basic and the $9 per barrel hypothesis. The $6 per barrel hypothesis is not shown and does not seem probable, especially since the present price of oil is not $9 but $11 a barrel.

---

4. OECD, *Energy Perspectives to 1985* (Paris, 1975).

FIGURE 4.2
Primary Energy Requirements of OECD Countries

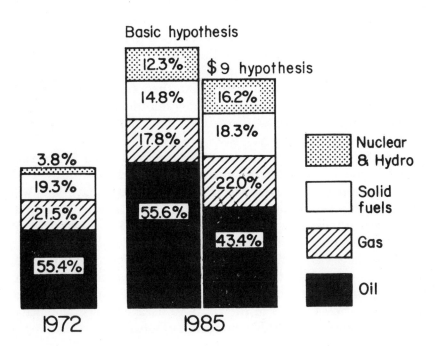

Source: OECD, "Study on Energy Perspectives until 1985" (Paris, 1975).

From the OECD estimates shown in Figure 4.2 it may be seen that oil, which in 1972 covered 55.4 percent of the total primary energy requirements of the OECD countries, is expected in 1980 to account for 57.4 percent according to the basic hypothesis and 47.3 percent if the $9 hypothesis is used. In 1985 the share is to be 55.6 percent under the first hypothesis and 43.4 percent under the second. The decline in the proportion of oil is to be offset by an increase in nuclear energy, which is to contribute 9.8 percent in 1980 and 16.2 percent in 1985, under the $9 hypothesis.

The same study estimates that the OECD area would produce in 1985 almost 80 percent of its energy requirements as compared with 65 percent in 1972. But these forecasts can change. They depend on such factors as economies in energy, economic recovery, and the possibility of developing national resources in each industrialized country.[5]

In fact, the very great increase in the price of oil now makes possible the exploitation of petroleum sources previously considered unprofitable. Technological progress now plays and will continue to play an important role in this field. It is believed that, through methods of tertiary recovery, a reduction in the cost of crude petroleum may take place.

On the basis of the estimates that now appear most reliable, the oil exports of the OPEC countries will increase until 1980 and will thereafter decline. Thus, the Morgan Guaranty Trust Co. foresees that by the end of the 1970-80 decade the world demand for oil (socialist and OPEC countries excluded) will increase by 9 million barrels a day, but the relative demand for oil from the

---

5. Energy forecasts in the United States are a typical example of these changes. Contrary to certain forecasts, production in the United States has continued to fall despite an increase in drilling. Moreover, the dependence of the United States on foreign supplies increased in 1976 as compared with 1975. According to a report by the Federal Energy Agency (July 1976), oil imports in 1976 would cost $35 billion instead of $27 billion for 1975. Furthermore, the same report confirms the downward revision of the estimate of the number of nuclear power stations to be constructed in coming years. The number will be 170 by 1985 instead of the 202 foreseen for 1975. The reduction results both from cost and environmental problems.

TABLE 4.7

World Oil Reserves at the End of 1974

Country/Region	Billions of Tons	Percent of Total	Billions of Barrels
United States	5.3	5.4	40.6
Canada	1.1	1.2	8.8
Caribbean	2.6	2.7	18.4
Other Western hemisphere	3.1	3.1	22.2
Total Western hemisphere	12.1	12.4	90.0
Western Europe	3.5	3.6	26.3
Middle East	55.0	56.3	403.4
Africa	9.1	9.3	68.3
USSR	11.4	11.6	83.4
Eastern Europe	0.4	0.4	3.0
China	3.4	3.5	25.0
Other Eastern hemisphere	2.8	2.9	21.0
Total Eastern hemisphere	85.6	87.6	630.4
World (except USSR, Eastern Europe, and China)	82.5	84.5	609.0
World	97.7	100.0	720.4

Source: British Petroleum Co., *Documentation* (1974).

OPEC countries is likely to increase by no more than 2 million barrels a day.[6] The difference will be covered by other sources of oil in the West and the East, including China, where the exploitation of oil resources is being expanded each year.[7]

---

6. Morgan Guaranty Trust Co., *World Financial Markets*, October 20, 1975.

7. It is estimated that in 1988 oil production in China will exceed 400 million tons annually, that is, the quantity now being produced by Saudi

According to other estimates, in 1990 global demand for oil will reach 160 million barrels a day, as compared with 1974 when it did not go beyond 90 million barrels a day. Thus in 1990 oil will still cover 50 percent of the energy needs of the world, as compared with 55 percent today. Consequently, it appears that its role will continue to be vital.

Moreover, world reserves of oil are an important factor (see Table 4.7). It is noteworthy that the largest share of reserves is located in the Middle East, which has 56.3 percent of the total. The USSR is in second place with 11.6 percent. Africa comes next with 9.3 percent, and North America has 6.6 percent.

Arabia. On the other hand, the oil reserves of the North Sea may be exploitable for the next 15 to 20 years using the techniques at present employed. *International Herald Tribune* (Paris), December 2, 1975.

5

THE UNDERLYING CAUSES OF THE CRISIS

THE INSUFFICIENCY OF PRODUCTIVE INVESTMENTS

The underlying cause of inflation and unemployment is, in the first instance, the insufficiency of productive investments. This insufficiency has the direct result of diminishing the supply of available goods and services. Inflation and unemployment are a consequence of the nonsatisfaction of overall demand.

Indeed, when the increase in overall demand is more rapid than the increase in supply, inflation begins. But if other factors are added, as has been the case since 1966—a lack of food products, monetary uncertainty, abrupt price increases, speculation—inflation is accentuated. Inflation is fed by a spiral rise in salaries and prices, as workers demand a readjustment of their wages to compensate for the increase in the cost of living. Meanwhile, entrepreneurs increase their prices to compensate for the wage increases. As a result, inflation becomes generalized and, through international trade, it becomes a worldwide problem that no single country can effectively solve.

Moreover, under the influence of various factors, inflation takes shape as a complex phenomenon characterized by: (1) inflation through spiral increases in costs of wages-prices-wages; (2) inflation caused by excess demand for strategic raw materials (demand inflation); (3) inflation due to increased prices for basic raw materials (cost inflation).

Nourished by a series of factors, inflation becomes chronic and, as a result of the behavior of different social groups, takes on its own dynamic with harmful effects on the economy and society. The initial unleashing of inflationary pressures begins when overall demand exceeds the short-term possibilities of the productive apparatus.

Justification for this interpretation is provided by the history of inflation in the United States. According to a study by *Business Week*,[1] inflation in the United States has evolved in the following way since 1966:

In 1966–69: The demand phase fed by the enormous deficits incurred to finance the Vietnam war. The economy was incapable of satisfying the additional demand generated by the increase of incomes.

In 1969–72: The period of cost-push inflation resulting from wage increases to compensate for the increased cost of living.

In 1973–74: A new period of inflation stimulated additionally by an increase in food product prices and then by the abrupt rise in oil prices.

An analysis of the history of American inflation since 1966 proves that the underlying cause of inflation and unemployment is an insufficiency of production, originating in a lack of investments. It is estimated that the Vietnam war cost about $300 billion from 1965 to 1973, when the Paris agreements were signed. The disequilibrium between supply and demand created the first disorder in the functioning of the market economy.

Inflation in the United States as in other countries has had the result of greatly reducing purchasing power. Between 1939 and 1975, the dollar lost 75 percent of its value, as is shown in Figure 5.1. Inflation is also the worst form of tax, weighing particularly on the poorest.

------

1. *Business Week*, June 1, 1974.

FIGURE 5.1   59

Purchasing Power of the U.S. Dollar

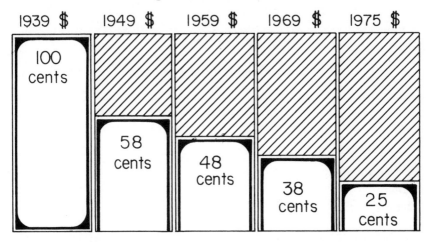

Source: U.S. Department of Labor.

The evolution of investments during recent years in the industrialized world (socialist countries excluded) confirms our view that the insufficiency of investments is the underlying cause of today's economic disorder.

Let us look at some figures. In the decade between 1960 and 1970 the gross national product of the Western industrial countries increased by $918 billion. Although $150 billion of this increase was absorbed during that decade by additional military expenses, a large amount remained, making possible an annual growth rate of about 5.5 percent and an inflation rate of 3.5 percent. With the zero growth of recent years, not only is there no longer any increase in national income to improve living standards but military expenditures are continually rising. Now we are confronted with a very sharp reduction in income available to take care of civilian needs, which should include needs arising from the increase in population.

Thus, recent years have seen an insufficiency of productive investments. In the industrialized countries since 1970—and here may be cited as one example the case of the nine countries of the Common Market—investments in fixed capital have represented a continuously declining proportion of GNP. The evolution of the volume of public and private investment (gross fixed capital formation) as a percentage of the figure for the preceding year is shown in Table 5.1.

TABLE 5.1

Gross Fixed Capital Formation

	Annual Percentage Changes	
Country	1974	1975
West Germany	−8.1	−6.75
France	+3.2	−4.50
Belgium	+8.0	−2.25
Italy	+4.2	−17.00
Switzerland	−8.1	−20.00
United Kingdom	−2.8	−1.50

Source: OECD, *Economic Outlook* 18 (Paris, December 1975).

The fact that national income is a function of the volume of investments is supported by the evolution of economic growth during the 1965–74 period. In this decade economic growth in France (4.2 percent) was greater than in West Germany (3.1 percent) and the United States (2.7 percent). According to a study prepared by the Paris Chamber of Commerce and Industry, these differences are explained "by the relatively great progress made by France in sustaining investment, as compared with the slow progress made in the two other countries."[2]

The experience of the past supports this thesis. Indeed, periods of stagnation always have been marked by low rates of capital formation. In the great depression of the 1930s, the rate of net capital formation in the United States fell to 1.4 percent of the national income between 1929 and 1938, as compared with 10 percent in 1921–29 and 13 to 16 percent before 1914.[3]

---

2. See *Le Monde*, December 30, 1975.

3. United Nations Economic Commission for Europe, *Survey of the Economic Situation in Europe in 1949* (Geneva, 1950), p. 229.

MILITARY EXPENDITURES

We are led to the recognition that all savings unused and all capital wasted (that is, capital not effectively mobilized for the development of world resources and the improvement of population well-being) must be considered as the essential and underlying cause of today's economic crisis. According to a study for the Arms Control Association, the Institute for World Order, and the Congress for Peace through Law, world military expenditures have increased in spite of the economic recession and inflation.[4] They amounted to $270 billion in 1974 and it is estimated that in 1975 the total was approximately $300 billion, an increase of 11.1 percent in a single year. On the other hand, the national income of the industrialized countries dropped by 2.1 percent during the same year.

Because of their fear of aggravating unemployment, the industrialized countries encourage the manufacture and export of arms. The commercial prospects for arms have never been as bright as they are today. It is astonishing to note that even political leaders long hostile to any extension of arms exports begin to see things otherwise. Even the workers in this sector demand the maintenance of employment through the development of arms exports. Thus, the expansion of the arms industry takes on disturbing dimensions and has unfavorable repercussions for both importing and exporting countries: for the importing countries because of the aggravation of their payments problems and the waste of capital; for the exporting countries because of the unbalanced use of their resources.[5]

First place among the arms-exporting countries is held by the United States, whose arms exports in the year 1974 are estimated at $8.3 billion. The Soviet Union is in second place with an export value of $5.5 billion, and France is in third place with 3 billion dollars. West Germany might now be added to this list, even though

---

4. See *International Herald Tribune* (Paris), March 2, 1976.

5. The Brooks report for the OECD, *Science, Growth, and Society—A New Perspective* (Paris, August 1971), emphasizes that the correlation between military expenditures and economic growth appears negative and that the pre-

TABLE 5.2

Military Expenditures as a Percentage of GNP in NATO Countries
(at present factor prices)

Country	1971	1973	1975[a]
Belgium	3.2	3.0	3.3
Denmark	2.9	2.5	2.9
France	4.7	4.4	4.6
West Germany	3.8	3.9	4.1
Greece	5.5	4.6	6.9
Italy	3.2	3.2	2.8
Luxembourg	0.9	0.9	1.0
Netherlands	3.8	3.7	3.9
Norway	4.0	3.7	3.9
Portugal	8.1	6.7	7.5
Turkey	4.9	4.4	7.0[b]
United Kingdom	5.8	5.6	5.7
NATO–Europe	4.3	4.2	4.3
Canada	2.7	2.3	2.4
United States	7.7	6.6	6.7
Total NATO	6.2	5.3	5.3

[a]Preliminary evaluation.
[b]Estimate.
Source: NATO, "Revue de NATO" 6 (Brussels, December 1975).

at the moment it is in sixth place with a modest sum of $100 million as a result of its controls on exports, for forces impelling it to increase its arms exports appear very strong.[6]

---

dominance of military research leads to a disequilibrium in the application of the results of research by creating serious bottlenecks in the economy.

6. On this subject, see the article in *Der Spiegel* of September 15, 1975 under the title "Waffen für die Welt?" This article was reproduced under the heading "The German Armaments Industry and the World Arms Market" in *Problèmes économiques*, March 10, 1976.

Table 5.2 shows the increasing size of military expenditures and their relationship to GNP during the last five years among the NATO (North Atlantic Treaty Organization) countries. Thus, the percentage of GNP absorbed by military expenditures is large and in some countries a great increase in this ratio is noted particularly between 1973 and 1975. As a result of the Cyprus crisis, the growth of military expenditures in Greece and Turkey has been very high, which will not fail to have unfavorable repercussions on these two countries' economic and social progress during coming years.

In the United States the increase in military expenditures in 1975 as compared with the previous year was 8.5 percent, while economic growth was 3.3 percent lower and the growth of industrial production 8.8 percent lower. It also may be added that private productive investments fell by 13.6 percent during the same period.

Furthermore, the report on the U.S. budget for the fiscal year 1977 indicates that a continuing increase is foreseen for coming years. Military expenditures over the five years 1977–81 would be as indicated in Table 5.3.

TABLE 5.3

Projected U.S. Military Expenditures, 1977–81

Year	Billions of Dollars	Annual Increase (in percentages)
1977	114.9	—
1978	122.4	6.5
1979	131.9	7.8
1980	141.6	7.4
1981	151.5	7.0
Total	662.3	

Source: The Budget of the United States Government, Fiscal Year 1977 (Washington, D.C., 1976), p. 35.

In France an annual increase of 14.5 percent in the defense budget is projected for the period 1977–82; this is about three times the rate of economic growth expected during the same period. It would appear that the annual increase in military expenditures will be much greater than that in GNP, for which a growth rate on the order of 5 percent is foreseen.

Meanwhile, the developing countries are devoting very large sums to their military expenditures at a time when they are confronted with priority needs for economic development. In many developing countries the share of military expenditures in total public expenditures is far greater than the corresponding percentage in the industrialized countries. Thus, as the magazine

TABLE 5.4

Armaments Sales by the United States
(in millions of dollars)

	1971	1973	1975
Developed Countries			
NATO	361.7	826.8	2,996.3
Others	193.3	151.2	302.2
All	555.0	978.0	3,298.5
Developing Countries			
Southern Africa	16.1	2.8	34.6
Latin America	49.4	111.1	154.3
Middle East and North Africa	928.1	2,948.8	5,508.3
Asia	90.7	238.8	484.2
All	1,084.3	3,301.5	6,181.4
of which: *OPEC Countries*	496.5	765.4	4,365.3
Total	1,639.3	4,279.5	9,479.9

Source: U.S. Defense Department, *Foreign Military Sales and Military Assistance Facts* (Washington, D.C., November 1974).

Der Spiegel express it, "the arms buyers are waiting in line." Especially the Arab countries, as well as other countries of the Third World, are seeking to strengthen their arsenals by buying aircraft, tanks, rockets, and ships—armaments that are increasingly costly as a result of technological progress. All precedents have been surpassed in the growth of strategic forces. According to information published by the Swedish International Peace Research Institute, the developing countries increased their arms purchases by 40 percent in 1974, spending $40 billion. Iran alone spent $3.8 billion on war material from the United States, while Saudi Arabia expects to buy arms valued at $25 billion in the years up to 1980.

A more precise picture of the unprecedented increase in military expenditures may be obtained from the statistics presented in Table 5.4, showing arms sales by the United States. It may be seen that arms sales to the developing countries increased six times between 1971 and 1975, reaching a total of $6 billion—including $4.3 billion from the OPEC countries.

This arms race does not contribute to true security, either nationally or for humanity as a whole. For, as the Algiers Colloquium correctly stated in June 1975: "There is a paradoxical link between the arms race and real security. The more that is spent on armaments the more the world becomes exposed to danger, for fewer resources are available to satisfy human needs."[7]

There is no doubt that the key to worldwide security lies in development. Misery and poverty in the most populated parts of the globe create insecurity for all. Moreover, in the present state of stagflation, the arms race accentuates inflationary pressures and aggravates the general economic crisis.

Confronted with this unproductive orientation, the least developed countries have found only one solution to keep their economies afloat and carry out at least part of their development programs: import of foreign capital. But wasting this borrowed capital in large part on military uses does not help their econo-

----

7. This colloquium, held in Algiers from June 24 to 27, 1975, was organized by the Center for International Development, whose seat is in Paris.

mies to overcome the present crisis or favor long-term economic progress.

UNEMPLOYMENT AND UNEMPLOYMENT BENEFITS

In addition to the elements already considered, another factor leading to unproductive use of the world's wealth should be borne in mind. This factor is unemployment insurance, as noted earlier. There is no doubt that unemployment benefits are socially indispensable; nobody can contest the need for them. Public authorities must grant relief to help those in need and to avoid violence, which otherwise would become inevitable. The question that arises is related to the consequences of unemployment benefits for economic activity, for inflation, and even for the level of unemployment.

The effects of such expenditures do not seem favorable. First, from the viewpoint of production, the economy loses the quantity of goods and services that could be produced by a utilization of the unemployed manpower. Is it possible to estimate the amount of this lost production?

We estimate the amount devoted to payment of unemployment insurance benefits by the western industrialized countries as being on the order of $25 billion for the 17 million who are unemployed. The United States alone, whose unemployed number almost 8 million, spent $17 billion for unemployment insurance benefits in 1975. The expenditures foreseen for 1976 amounted to $19.4 billion.

The other industrialized countries also have large supports to the unemployed; benefits may vary between 70 and 90 percent of wages for those receiving unemployment payments.

If $25 billion were used for productive purposes, what would be the effects on the increase of incomes? The OECD has tried to estimate the potential order of magnitude of the international multiplier effects that would be realized if all industrialized countries adopted expansionist measures at the same time. The results, calculated through use of the STEP econometric evaluation model, indicate a domestic multiplier factor for the average

OECD country of 1.75. This means that an autonomous injection of $1 billion in such an economy would increase the GNP by $1.75 billion if the effects in that country alone were taken into account. If account is taken of the international multiplier mechanism, the increase in GNP would be more than $2.5 billion.[8]

If we make a conservative estimate of the international multiplier factor, such as one to two, it may be said that a productive use of the sum of $25 billion at present expended on unemployment benefits would make it possible to increase GNP by about $50 billion.

But this is not all. The sum of $25 billion is not only removed from the machinery of production; it is also used in an unproductive way, thus engendering additional inflationary pressures and increasing inflation still more.

In addition, some economists argue that unemployment insurance leads to other economic distortions, resulting in an increase of unemployment. Indeed Martin Feldstein, the Harvard University economist, has advanced the thesis that unemployment insurance encourages recipients to remain unemployed longer than they should while permitting enterprises more easily to drop workers from the payroll.[9] Furthermore, according to Feldstein, the unemployment benefits paid—which are not subject to income taxes—have the effect of prolonging the duration of the search for new employment, which means a loss of output and results in social waste. He estimates that the present U.S. unemployment insurance benefits system results in an increase of 1.25 percent in the unemployment rate.

If the Feldstein thesis is valid, the present system of unemployment benefits has negative effects even on employment. Furthermore, the system has other important negative effects: instead of promoting policies aimed at economic growth, the present system creates economic distortions, which maintain and prolong the coexistence of inflation and unemployment.

---

8. See OECD *Observer* (Paris) no. 79 (January-February 1976) and *Perspectives Economiques* no. 18 (December 1975).

9. An analysis of this problem by Martin Feldstein may be found in *Business Week*, November 17, 1975.

CHAPTER

6

INVESTMENTS ON
AN INTERNATIONAL SCALE:
TOWARD A
POST-KEYNESIAN ERA?

THE INEFFECTIVENESS OF NATIONAL MEASURES

The underlying cause of the present economic crisis is, as we have already pointed out, an insufficiency of productive investments. The fact that governments have not taken this essential factor into account explains why their measures to promote economic recovery have not brought satisfactory results.

Indeed the joint efforts of national economic and monetary authorities, as well as international institutions, to try to overcome the increasing dangers of stagflation and deficits in current payments balances have had disappointing results.

In seeking to prevent the movement of the pendulum toward recession at one moment and inflation at another—according to the degree of gravity with which each problem was posed—the governments have been led to adopt measures that very often were contradictory. Also, incompatibility between the measures taken has inevitably reduced their effectiveness.

Similar efforts have been made by international bodies, which have tried to coordinate their actions. The leaders of the international bodies have attempted to stop the march of stagflation, to reduce its negative effects on fragile economies, and to contribute to the search for a solution to balance-of-payments problems. In the framework of these efforts, special funds have been created. At the same time, mechanisms and payments terms for loans to developing countries have been modified.

The measures taken until now have had common features in spite of their great diversity—they were limited to the short term, they failed to take into account the totality of the world economies, they failed to include an effective policy for large-scale investments. Efforts to find an economic regulator limited in time and in space have been repeated many times without success. This failure confirms that the present crisis cannot be considered simply as cyclical since it reflects problems that call for profound structural reform in the economic system.

The failure of the measures taken has been pointed out by experts of international organizations. Two economists of the International Labour Office, D. Friedman and R. Broadfield, have studied the social and economic costs of inflation in the United Kingdom and the United States in 1965–75. They say the various efforts to hold back inflation caused an increase in unemployment. On the other hand, accelerated inflation and the increasing burden of fiscal charges have led to a general decline in real personal income, despite large wage increases. Moreover, increases in the cost of living have reduced the real value of wages and salaries. These conclusions, which relate to the whole Western world affected by inflation, are confirmed by the OECD.[1]

Speaking before the ECOSOC session of the United Nations on July 7, 1975, OECD Secretary General Emile van Lennep underlined the fact that, both during the business cycle boom of and the cyclical recession phase of 1974–75, governments made mistakes in their anticyclical policies:

Governments were too late in taking action to prevent the excessively high upswing of 1973, and when subsequently the increase in oil prices was added to other inflationary elements they underestimated the power and the persistence of the recessionary movement.

---

1. See ILO, *The World of Labor and Development* (February 1976).

Indeed, as long as business circles and consumers remain convinced of the persistence of inflation, any monetary and budgetary policy undertaken to combat inflation becomes ineffective; it can only stimulate economic activity at the price of reinforcing inflation. Even the president of the Council of Governors of the U.S. Federal Reserve Bank, Arthur Burns, in a study published in the magazine *Challenge* (January-February 1976) reached the conclusion that too much reliance has been put on monetary and budgetary policies as a means of stimulating economic activity. In his opinion, when inflationary anticipations continue to develop, as at present, classic anti-inflationary measures should be used only with great prudence.

Certain factors have sown disorder, but it is undeniable that the present crisis cannot be considered as cyclical in origin. The signs of weakness are important, for they toll the bells for a past epoch and announce the coming of a new international economic and social order.

We observe that the industrialized countries are undergoing a period of recession characterized by progressive reduction of investments, disturbing unemployment, excessive inflation, and monetary disorder unprecedented during the postwar period. Faced with this climate of uncertainty, consumers hold back their expenditures. The result is a hypertrophy of savings, which aggravates the recession.

Indeed, certain phenomena of the present recession have disagreeably surprised governments and forecasting institutes. For instance, the attitude of savers has contradicted the thesis that inflation results in a reduction of the proportion of income saved. The prevailing thesis has been that acceleration of inflation would cause a "flight from money." On the contrary, the experience of the two past years has shown that the erosion of the value of assets and the desire to have funds immediately available stimulated inflation. In all countries, a clear increase in the volume of savings is observed. Even individuals are saving an ever larger proportion of income as inflation accelerates.[2] The high rate of in-

---

2. An interesting analysis of this phenomenon is made by Anthony Harris in the *Financial Times* (London), September 12, 1975.

crease in bank deposits is a partial indication of this tendency. Table 6.1 shows the growth of bank deposits between 1974 and 1975.

Table 6.2 shows that the rate of growth in savings deposits more than doubled between 1974 and 1975 in all industrialized countries except West Germany and Belgium. The result has been an excess of inactive savings rather than a conversion of savings into investments. As a consequence, unemployment has grown at an increasingly rapid pace.

TABLE 6.1

Percentage Increases in Bank Savings Deposits

	Between 1973 and 1974	Between 1974 and 1975
West Germany	12.4	19.8
France	7.8	31.7
Italy	3.9	28.0
Netherlands	4.3	15.2
Belgium	9.2	14.5
Luxembourg	5.3	18.0

Source: Eurostat, October 1975.

THE KEYNESIAN THEORY AND TODAY'S CRISIS

Do these developments justify the explanation for the crisis given by the Keynesian theory? Keynes, in *The General Theory of Employment, Interest and Money*, published in 1936, gave a realistic interpretation—contrary to the classical one—of the functioning of the economy. According to Keynes, the full employment of the factors of production is not brought about by automatic market mechanisms as the classical economists argued but by "effective demand," which determines production.

In the final analysis, effective demand is formed by the two possible uses of income—consumption and investment. Further, according to Keynes, income depends on the volume of employment: When employment increases, global income also increases.

Consequently, an increase in the volume of total income will result in increased consumption and savings, engendering investment. The volume of employment is determined by both the propensity to consume and the volume of new investments. The result is that, if these two elements of effective demand are sufficient to provide dynamism for the labor market, full employment is ensured. Conversely, if effective demand is insufficient, the level of employment will be lower, the factors of production will not be fully utilized and workers will not have jobs; this is how unemployment comes about.

According to Keynes, economic equilibrium presupposes that total income will be expended through consumption and investment. Consequently, if one part of the population limits its consumption expenditures, then to safeguard the economic equilibrium of the market other persons must acquire additional purchasing power to absorb the excess production. If this does not occur, the reduction in demand will lead to a drop in production and result in underemployment.

Savings formation also can lead to underemployment in certain circumstances. Keynes holds that in order for the economy to be in equilibrium, there must be an equalization between savings and investment. However, each time the volume of savings increases more than the volume of investments (that is, when a certain amount of income saved remains unused and is not converted into investment), there is a negative influence on effective demand, on production, and on the level of employment. Thus, inactive savings create unemployment. Therefore, economic equilibrium depends on the behavior of the economic actors.

Is the Keynesian theory confirmed by the actual experience of the recession? Since 1973 we have witnessed a decline of production in the developed countries. A sharp drop in investments has left savings in the industrialized countries unused and inactive. Because of the persistence of the recession, of inflationary pressures, and of unemployment, entrepreneurs do not foresee substantial profits and, since the marginal profitability of capital is declining, they hesitate to make new investments in their production apparatus.

We thus enter a vicious circle of economic disequilibrium, leading to a road without an exit, a road with unemployment and inflation as its main signposts. Hesitation to invest is widespread today in almost all countries. According to the U.S. Department of Commerce, a decline in investments by U.S. companies was expected in 1976 for the second consecutive year. Real investments, already 10 percent lower in 1975 than in 1974, would drop a further 5 percent. Even a decline of investments in current prices was foreseen.[3] It may also be noted that in most countries of Europe, and in France more particularly, gross investment (which in 1973 showed an increase of 5.6 percent over the preceding year) dropped by 4.9 percent in 1975 as compared with 1974. In French private industry the decline in 1975 was 10 percent, while in agriculture, transport, and trade it was 15 percent.[4]

The situation is becoming even more serious, for it appears that private entrepreneurs hesitate to make new investments, even when the state grants numerous investment advantages (loans at reduced rates of interest, fiscal advantages). With respect to this very point, the opinion of an important Swiss bank may be cited: "An uncertainty unknown since the thirties prevails in business enterprises and adversely affects their current decisions. If it continues, it could finally undermine the foundations of the free enterprise economy."[5]

Characteristic of the confusion that reigns in most industrialized countries is the situation in the United Kingdom, the motherland of the father of the full employment theory. The British government, in order to cope with the inflation problem, has decided to reduce public expenditures by large amounts—which

---

3. We would cite particularly the investment reductions in telecommunications (3.5 percent), mining industries (4 percent), railroads (10 percent), and air transport companies (3 percent).

4. See *L'Expansion* (Paris), January 1976, p. 68.

5. Union Bank of Switzerland, *Bulletin*, October 1975.

is completely contrary to the Keynesian theory—and to leave to private enterprise the initiative for making large productive investments. However, because the chancellor of the Exchequer decided to increase by 2 percent the employers' contributions for social security, the Confederation of British Industry, representing the employers, declared to Prime Minister James Callaghan that they would not launch an investment campaign, thus upsetting the climate of confidence needed for economic recovery.[6]

How can the vacuum created by inactive savings be filled? We must free ourselves from the classical theories according to which saving precedes investment and is the basic factor determining development. According to modern theory, it is investment that creates income and thereby engenders savings.

Thus, during underemployment, when the state decides to carry out public works even at a time of inflation, by utilizing inactive savings, new income is created and is divided into expenditures for consumption and for further savings. The result is that the unemployed who are given jobs will buy more, thereby providing additional income for producers. In turn, producers will spend and save more, also creating additional income. This is how the multiplier plays a role, for its effects are a function of the propensity to consume.

Under present conditions it must be acknowledged that employment depends on expenditure, which can be used for consumption and for investment. If these two factors—that is, the propensity to consume and the amount of investment—constitute an effective demand sufficient to absorb the supply of labor, full employment is ensured.

This is the keystone of the Keynesian theory. If, on the contrary, effective demand is insufficient, then production capacity will remain unused and massive unemployment will result. If this happens, we will have a deficiency of demand, which is the main cause of unemployment and inflation.

---

6. See *The Times* (London), July 31, 1976. On the economic problem of the United Kingdom, see also R. Bacon and W. Eltis, *Britain's Economic Problem: So Few Producers* (London, Macmillan, 1976).

THE CRITICISMS OF THE KEYNESIAN THEORY.

The full employment policy is being contested by two great economists of the classical school, Friedrich von Hayek and Jacques Rueff, who opposed the Keynesian theory when it was applied in the years 1935–40 and have returned to their criticism with new arguments. In a 1976 study von Hayek emphasizes that "unemployment today is the direct and inevitable consequence of the so-called full-employment policies pursued during the past twenty five years." He adds, "The present economic crisis also severely undermines the authority of political economy, or at least marks the collapse of the Keynesian illusion which has been the fashion for a generation."[7]

For his part Jacques Rueff, in two articles published in *Le Monde*, renews his old disagreement with Keynes on the basis of the present economic crisis. According to Rueff, unemployment is due to the artificial maintenance of real wages at levels too high in relation to the general price level. He also states: "The doctrine of full employment has opened wide the flood-gates of inflation and unemployment" and "it is about to destroy before our eyes what remains of Western civilization."[8]

Are these criticisms of the Keynesian theory justified?

When Keynes formulated his theory of the equivalence between savings and investment, he probably meant productive investments. He argued that when private enterprise was reluctant to make new investments the state should intervene by adopting appropriate policies to activate unused savings and to encourage the propensity to consume of the economically weaker classes. Keynes envisaged especially investments aimed at the increase of goods and services that were useful and indispensable for the

---

7. Large extracts from this study, which was submitted to a symposium organized by a private U.S. firm, Monex International, were reproduced in an article by Paul Fabra. See *L'Année économique et sociale 1975, la crise*, published by *Le Monde* (Paris, January 1976), p. 151.

8. *Le Monde*, February 19, 20, and 21, 1976. See also Alain Barrère et al., *Controversies over the Keynes System* (Paris: Economica Publishing House, 1975).

population, and not the production of means of destruction such as armaments. The production of armaments, as already explained, takes away a large part of the national income, which should be used in its entirety for economic and social development.

During the first 25 postwar years, the Keynesian theory remained valid and its application made possible the maintenance of full employment in the industrialized countries of Western Europe, even though some unproductive expenditures were made. This period saw a sustained growth unprecedented in history, while inflation did not exceed 3.5 percent a year, and unemployment was less than 2 percent, despite the need to employ 2 million immigrant workers.

But there are limits to any policy. Disequilibrium is created from the moment when there is lack of rational policy coordination, when national resources are wasted on unproductive goods, and when changes in economic and social conditions are ignored. Inflation then becomes excessive and unemployment is inevitable. This happened during 1973-76 when production dropped, savings remained inactive, investments fell, unemployment took on disturbing dimensions, and new problems arose on the national and international levels. To this extent, it may be said that there is a certain element of truth in the criticisms of von Hayek and Rueff.

But this disequilibrium cannot be attributed to the Keynesian theory: the cause was rather the irrationality of those who tried to apply it. It is irrational to try to apply a policy without taking into consideration the new endogenous and exogenous factors that have appeared in the economy and society. Any theory requires readjustment. Keynes himself never consider his theory unchangeable. When asked about its contribution to the economy, he gave this significant reply: "I have given capitalism 30 years of reprieve, of further life."

However, it is a fact that governments and the experts who advise them are confused. They do not want to recognize the profound changes in the structure of the world economy. They do not dare to see or to confront reality face to face, to decide upon and adopt a rational and new global economic strategy. Alfred Sauvy is entirely right when he writes that "the economic troubles, the ailments from which the Western countries are suffering, and the misfortunes which threaten them, have the same origin: an immense social cowardice, a fear of acting, a fear of speaking, a fear of seeing and even a fear of thinking."[9]

Thus, contrary to the argument of von Hayek, if Keynes had lived longer he would have reexamined and enlarged his doctrine, adjusting it to the evolution of conditions so it could be applied on a worldwide scale. As early as 1953, in *Planning and Social Progress*, I wrote: "The idea must not be excluded that if Keynes were living today he would make a further advance with regard to the responsibility for full employment. The application of his theory imposes precisely on the state a very large initiative in the conduct of economic activity."[10]

TOWARD A POST-KEYNESIAN ERA

Under present conditions, when each industrial country finds itself in a vicious circle of inflation and unemployment, no single country can resolve the crisis or create sustained growth. It is possible that the policy of full employment in the industrialized countries has reached and even surpassed the limits of application. Technological progress has created new conditions that require enlargement of the Keynesian theory. New conditions on the labor market, the social policy adopted with respect to the unemployed, the environment, pollution, the confirmed widening of the gap between the rich and poor countries, polycentrism in international politics—all these factors require new ways of thinking about economic and social problems. These have now become world problems. No country can presently succeed in combating inflation, and no policy can be effective in achieving economic and social progress, without taking into consideration the interdependence of all economies, of both the industrialized countries

---

9. Alfred Sauvy, *L'Economie du Diable, chômage et inflation* (Paris: Calman-Levy, 1976), p. 7.

10. Angelos Angelopoulos, *Planisme et progrès social* (Paris: Librairie Générale, 1953), p. 125.

and the developing countries. Consequently, if a policy of full employment is to be effective, it must be extended to wider horizons—to productive and useful goals on a worldwide scale.

For these reasons, large productive investments must be made not only in the industrialized countries—in order to supply the equipment needed by the developing countries—but also in the developing countries in order to utilize this equipment for the development of national resources. In this way, effective demand would be created on an international scale, capable of progressively eliminating inflation and absorbing unemployment, while contributing to an increase in income. The OECD estimate demonstrates that the multiplier effects of an initial expenditure are almost doubled if the expenditure is made in a synchronized manner on an international scale instead of being carried out by a single country. As we have already said, the OECD econometric model study shows that the value of the domestic multiplier for an average OECD country is about 1.75, whereas if the international multiplier mechanism is taken into account the average effect on economic activity in each country could be higher than 2.5. This is an additional argument in favor of a broader interpretation of the Keynesian theory.

From this viewpoint, Keynes may be considered as the precursor of the new international economic order for which all countries today are necessarily striving. Indeed, the Keynesian doctrine should be interpreted not in the narrow framework of one nation—as was justified right after World War II—but rather in the light of new factors, and of the evolution of the economy and society on a worldwide scale. Perhaps Jacques Rueff had already perceived this inevitable mutation when in 1947 he formulated this significant prognosis: "Because of Lord Keynes, the next cyclical crisis will be a time of profound political changes, changes which certain people hope for and others fear."

By thus enlarging the application of the Keynesian theory not only to the role of the state but also to the competency of the entire international community, we may speak of the beginning of the post-Keynesian era.

This new epoch should signify an orientation toward a profound change in ideas and institutions, an abandonment of the policy followed until now, which has been aimed only at the maintenance of old and outmoded structures, and the adoption of a new forward-looking constructive policy. Such a policy would make possible the establishment of a global model for resource use and the satisfaction of the needs of humanity; it would combat misery and poverty, and would permanently improve the living standards and cultural levels of all peoples.

7

GUIDELINES FOR
A NEW INTERNATIONAL
ECONOMIC ORDER

APPLYING THE IDEA OF PROSPERITY
ON AN INTERNATIONAL SCALE

Analysis of the economic situation leads us to the conclusion that the present deep and generalized crisis makes it necessary to draw up a coordinated action program. This program should include changes in the structure of the world institutional system and the recognition of certain essential principles. These principles are indispensable for the speedy inauguration of a global strategy aimed at economic and social progress on an international scale.

For the formulation of a new international development strategy, it is necessary to start from the following principles:

1. The admission that prosperity is indivisible and that the rich countries will not be able to survive in the long run as islands in an ocean of misery. It must be recognized that economic development is an international responsibility. This viewpoint has been adopted by the United Nations General Assembly, which has emphasized that "economic and social progress is a common responsibility, which should be shared by the international community as a whole."

2. A larger, more equitable, and more human conception should be given to the idea of development. The objective of development consists not only of the accumulation of goods but also and primarily of the promotion of the interests of the human being as an integral whole. Development is thus a process of structural change in economic, social, political, and cultural domains. Development must be carried out for the benefit of all and not of a small minority. It is a collective effort and its fruits must be equitably distributed among all who participate.

3. The adoption toward the poor countries of the same policy that the developed states apply on the national level with regard to their disfavored classes, that is, the notion of a welfare state that aims to improve the living conditions of the poor through a redistribution of national income, should be introduced on an international scale.

If humanity is to survive and progress in a climate of prosperity and peace, a new way of thinking must be adopted. We must liberate ourselves from outdated ideas, understand the revolutionary spirit of our epoch, and apply a new policy based on the principle of international solidarity, on the idea that prosperity is indivisible and that all people share in a single community. Otherwise, it will be difficult to avoid violence.

Worldwide economic and social progress can be ensured through sincere, constructive cooperation among all countries of the world to bring about profound changes in the economic and social structure. In her book *The Rich Nations and the Poor Nations*, economist Barbara Ward has said, "History teaches us that changes of such amplitude have sometimes been brought about through dialogue and cooperation, sometimes by a direct and violent confrontation, but most often by a mixture of confrontation and cooperation." Those who benefit from a system tend to be stubborn in refusing to make changes. But others believe that nothing will change without a total overturn. "When this stage of polarization is reached," adds Barbara Ward, "dialogue is impossible and violence becomes inevitable, unless a way is found to go beyond the stage of egoism and to discover together a community of interest."[1]

---

1. Barbara Ward, *The Rich Nations and the Poor Nations* (New York: Norton, 1972).

Thus in the framework of a new international economic order,[2] of which we shall speak in more detail further on, augmented co-operation is of value for all countries, developed or developing.

SHORT- AND LONG-TERM OBJECTIVES

Such cooperation would lead to the establishment of an international development strategy, which should contain both short- and long-term objectives.

The short-term objectives should be:

1. Realization of large-scale and productive investments, especially in the developing countries, which can also stimulate economic activity in the industrialized countries and worldwide.

2. Creation of a system to finance on especially favorable terms an acceleration of economic growth in the developing and developed countries, through the intermediary of an international organization.

3. Reinforcement of effective demand to absorb the output of additional goods and services, creating new jobs and eliminating unemployment.

4. Equitable regulation of the problem of raw materials, taking into account the interests of the producing countries and the industrialized countries.

5. Reinforcement of cooperation between all countries in trade, industry, science, and technology so as to increase the productive capacity of developing countries and of all countries.

The long-term objectives should be:

1. To accelerate economic and social progress in the developing countries, a decisive element for the world economy as a whole.

---

2. C. F. Bergsten, *Towards a New International Order* (Lexington, Mass.: D.C. Heath and Company, 1975), and Saul H. Mendlowitz, *On the Creation of*

2. To remove the injustice and inequality from which a large part of humanity suffers.

3. To reduce and then eliminate the immense gap separating the poor countries from the rich countries, a gap that increases each day to the detriment of the poorest countries.

Only the application of such policy, coordinating in a rational and effective way short- and long-term objectives, can contribute to a true recovery of the international economy and promote peace and security. Only such a policy can help bring about a new international economic order and the application of the Charter of the Rights and Duties of States called for in the resolution adopted by the Seventh Special Session of the United Nations General Assembly on September 18, 1975.

To apply this new development policy, two measures of major importance are needed: (1) to effectuate within each country large productive investments carried out by the state and public authorities and (2) to strengthen the propensity to consume by applying an appropriate incomes policy and concurrently to increase effective demand through new investments.

To attain this double objective, each country must create a specialized body charged with undertaking public sector investments while stimulating investment initiatives by the private sector. By drawing up a long-term plan, the state should commit itself to implementing a dynamic program for the realization of large-scale productive public works and for the satisfaction of collective needs. Such an undertaking would set in motion, through the multiplier effect, a series of forces favoring international development.

In order to. revive economic activity on an international scale, the governments and the United Nations should create a special development fund to finance development programs in the countries of the Third World, especially the poorest countries. We will discuss later the appropriate procedures to enable such an institution to fulfill its mission and to deal with the problem of financing.

---

a Just World Order (New York: Institute for World Order, 1976).

THE CHARTER OF THE ECONOMIC
RIGHTS AND DUTIES OF STATES

The role of the Third World is crucial if a new international development strategy is to be adopted by the United Nations. The crisis of recent years has contributed a strengthening of tendencies encouraging the adoption of a new policy. For a long time, these tendencies remained latent. But the success of the oil embargo and the spectacular increase of oil prices have shown that the countries producing basic products can make their claims prevail.

The texts of three documents, elaborated collectively by the countries of the Third World, merit attention in the framework of a search for a new international development policy and the adoption of a new international economic order:

1. The Charter of the Economic Rights and Duties of States, an instrument proposed by President Luis Echeverria of Mexico.

2. The Algiers Resolution (February 1975) of the Group of 77 proposed by Algerian President Houari Boumedienne, a resolution used as a basic document in the discussions at Lima.

3. The Lima Declaration on development and industrial co-operation, including a plan of action, adopted at the UNIDO Conference (March 1975).

From these proposals originated two resolutions on international economic development approved by the United Nations General Assembly: The Charter of the Economic Rights and Duties of States and the adoption of a "New International Economic Order."

The Charter of the Economic Rights and Duties of States is the outgrowth of a serious confrontation between the underdeveloped and the rich countries. In the course of its elaboration, a fundamental opposition between these two groups became apparent.

At the third session of UNCTAD held in Santiago in April 1972, Mexican President Luis Echeverria took the initiative of presenting a proposal for a Charter of the Economic Rights and

Duties of States. The fundamental objective was the establishment of a just economic order through the creation of a code regularizing economic relations between all states on principles of equity, justice, sovereign equality, interdependence, common interests, and cooperation among all without distinction between economic and social systems.

The initiative of the president of Mexico was favorably received. Resolution 45/3 approved by UNCTAD on May 18, 1972, with 90 votes in favor, none opposed, and 19 abstentions, set up a working group composed of representatives of 31 (and subsequently 40) states to elaborate a draft charter to protect the rights of all countries, and in particular of the developing countries.

The determination and the continuous efforts of President Echeverria and of the Group of 40 made it possible to arrange a unified position with the Group of 77 developing countries (whose votes in the United Nations have increased in number from 77, their size when the group was founded, to 123. In 1974 final approval of the text was obtained.

Thus, at the celebrated twenty-ninth session of the United Nations General Assembly held from September 17 to December 18, 1974, the Charter of the Economic Rights and Duties of States was adopted by a large majority (120) despite the opposition or reluctance of the rich countries (six voted against and ten abstained). The same General Assembly adopted a resolution instituting a "new international economic order."

It is useful to mention here some principles of the charter concerning the fundamental elements of international economic relations:

1. Each state has the sovereign and inalienable right to choose its economic system as well as its political, social, and cultural system in conformity with the will of its people, without external interference, pressure, or threats of any kind.

2. Each state maintains and freely exercises entire and permanent sovereignty over all its wealth, natural resources, and

economic activities, including the right to possess, utilize and dispose of them as it chooses.

3. Each state has the right:

• To regulate foreign investments within the limits of its national jurisdiction and to exercise its authority over these investments in conformity with its laws and regulations and with its own priorities and national objectives. No state will be obliged to grant privileged treatment to foreign investments.

• To regulate and to control the activities of transnational companies within the limits of its national jurisdiction and to take measures to ensure that these activities are in harmony with its economic and social policy. Transnational companies will not intervene in the internal affairs of the host state.

• To nationalize, expropriate, or transfer property rights over foreign assets, and in this event to pay an adequate indemnity, taking into account its laws and regulations and all circumstances it judges to be relevant. In all cases where the question of indemnification gives rise to differences, these will be settled in conformity with the internal legislation of the state that adopts such nationalization measures and by the tribunals of that state, unless all the states concerned freely agree to explore other peaceful means of resolving the differences on the basis of the sovereign equality of states and in conformity with the principle of a free choice of means of settlement.

According to the charter, the objective of these rights and duties is: to attain greater prosperity in all countries, with higher living standards for all peoples; to promote, through action by the entire international community, economic and social progress in all countries, and in particular in the developing countries.

COHERENT AND DYNAMIC
ECONOMIC COOPERATION

The success of the policy incorporated in the new international economic order and the Charter of the Economic Rights and Duties of States depends above all on sincere and effective cooperation between the industrialized countries and the developing countries.

However, the adoption of the resolutions on the charter and the new international order—which constitute a real economic decolonization—aroused an adverse reaction from the industrialized countries. The policy followed since the adoption of these resolutions also shows that the spirit of international economic cooperation has not yet been embodied in mutual understanding. The successive summit meetings held during 1975 and 1976 to examine the international economic situation further demonstrate—as we have already emphasized—a lack of elementary agreement among the countries concerned. The dialogue threatens to become a conflict.

Against a background of economic recession, a series of international conferences during 1975 and 1976 proved unsuccessful. UNIDO ended in Lima on March 27, 1975, without any change in the positions of the two camps. In April 1975 in Paris, on the occasion of the first preparatory meeting for the North-South dialogue convened at the invitation of President Giscard d'Estaing, it was hoped that the positions might draw closer. On September 1, 1975, then U.S. Secretary of State Henry Kissinger opened the seventh special session of the United Nations General Assembly with a conciliatory speech in which he proposed to "stabilize total export receipts" of the Third World countries. The second preparatory North-South meeting, October 13–16, 1975, opened the way for a dialogue and the commissions decided to meet in May 1976 at the Nairobi Conference.

The fourth UNCTAD session, May 5–31, 1976, in Nairobi, opened in a climate of skepticism. When the representatives of the 153 participating governments assembled, the Group of 77 charged that the United States and Europe had failed to fulfill their elementary obligations of solidarity toward the developing countries.

In comparison with the preceding UNCTAD meetings at New Delhi in 1968 and Santiago in 1972, which ended in failure, the fourth UNCTAD was on balance favorable since it resulted in a compromise, but without resolving the main problems.

Despite these difficulties, all recognized that international cooperation is an overriding necessity. The seventh special session of the United Nations General Assembly as well as the fourth UNCTAD examined a series of problems relating to international trade, basic materials, industrialization, transfer of science and technology, financing, food, and the monetary system. We will now indicate the main recommendations on those problems made at the conferences, except the recommendations on financing and the monetary system, which will be examined separately in a subsequent chapter.

Certain measures must be taken to ameliorate the terms of trade for the developing countries, to eliminate their chronic current account deficits and to restore an equitable relationship between the prices of exports and imports.

Processing raw materials in developing countries will both serve their national interests and further international economic cooperation. Concrete agreements aimed at reducing the instability of export payments and receipts are in the interest of the countries that produce as well as those that consume raw materials. The structure of payments must be revised.

In Nairobi, at the Fourth Conference of the UNCTAD, an integrated program was proposed, anticipating the study of and, by the end of 1978, the negotiation of separate accords on raw materials. Also foreseen was the discussion, followed by negotiations beginning in March 1977, of a General Fund charged with coordinating the financing of stockpiles.

Among other things, the Lima declaration for a Plan of Action assumes that the international community will move to encourage industrialization in the developing countries.

To this end, the United Nations Sixth Special Session has formulated certain measures, such as:

1. The developed countries must respond positively to the requests from the developing countries for financing industrial projects.

2. The developed countries should encourage private investment in the developing countries for the financing of industrial projects, especially those aimed at production for export.

3. With a view toward establishment of a new international division of labor, the developed countries and international institutions should contribute to the implantation of new industrial capacity in the developing countries producing raw materials, giving priority to the transformation of raw materials and basic products.

The problem of the industrialization of the developing countries is closely linked with the transfer of technology, a question that has become controversial. For some, technological transfer appears to be a magic formula capable of solving all the problems of development; for others, it constitutes an instrument of domination that reinforces the dependence of the developing countries on the industrial powers, especially through the intermediary of multinational companies.[3]

What emerges from this controversy is that technology constitutes an important factor in development and that the countries of the Third World must use it in a rational manner to accelerate their development. Their technological infrastructure should be reinforced by coordinated international cooperation. An international code of conduct for the transfer of technology to meet the needs of the developing countries is to be elaborated, so that these countries can benefit from easy and extensive access to technology. To reach this goal, operational programs for technical assistance should be pursued and intensified with the help of the developed countries and international organizations; these programs should center on formation of high-level national experts, including professional training.

---

3. The magazine *Tiers-Monde* devoted a special issue (January-March 1976) to an examination of this problem in studies made under the direction of Dimitri Germidis.

Multinational Companies

In the transfer of technology and industrialization, the multinational companies can play an important role on condition that their activity takes place in accordance with a code of conduct reflecting the interests of both parties. To make this role constructive, the multinational enterprises should: (1) respect the policies of the host governments in employment, social relations, social progress, environmental protection, and development; (2) supply governments and the public with information on their activities and policies; (3) abstain from all irregular activities with respect to national economic life, from all attempts to corrupt, and from all interference in political life.

These directing principles, adopted by various international organizations and representatives of the trade unions and employers of the OECD countries, constitute the essential elements of a code of contact for transnational enterprises so their activities are beneficial for the developing countries. The fourth UNCTAD (May 1976) adopted a resolution calling for a control over the activities of multinational enterprises.[4]

One recommendation adopted by the seventh special session of the United Nations General Assembly calls for reinforcement of cooperation among developing countries. The developed countries and the United Nations bodies are asked to encourage by all means a reciprocal cooperation at the subregional, regional, and inter-regional levels, through the creation of the appropriate institutional arrangements. In the framework of the United Nations system, the competent organs are to offer their support for such projects and to carry out new studies aimed at finding the best solutions for: (1) use of the theoretical and practical knowledge, natural resources, techniques, and funds available in the developing countries; (2) liberalization of trade, including payments and

---

4. See especially the United Nations study, *Multinational Companies and World Development* (New York, 1973), as well as the studies of the OECD, particularly the Declaration of June 21, 1976 of the member countries on "International Investment and Multinational Enterprises."

compensation agreements; and (3) transfer of technology from one developing country to another.

The Demographic Explosion and the Food Problem

The food problem is of priority urgency, especially in light of the demographic explosion that constitutes the gravest problem of our time. According to United Nations forecasts, the world population in 1976 was 4 billion and will be on the order of 6.5 billion in the year 2000. This enormous population increase will be added to a world where two-thirds of the people are badly nourished, badly housed, and badly clothed, and are deprived of medical care—thus compounding a situation that is already alarming.

The solution to the food problem lies mainly in the rapid increase of agricultural production in the developing countries. This requires radical modification of production structures and the trade in food. The developed countries must greatly increase their assistance to agriculture in the developing world and facilitate access to their markets for agricultural and food products, whether processed or unprocessed, exported from the developing countries.

More particularly, the developed countries should:

1. Ensure a sufficient supply of fertilizer to the developing countries and help them establish, over the long term, their local fertilizer production industries.

2. Encourage research by supporting international agricultural research centers and reinforcing the links between their national research institutions and the international centers, as well as the national centers in the developing countries.

In this way, all countries should cooperate in an international undertaking aimed at world food security.

8

THE TRANSFER OF GNP FROM
INDUSTRIALIZED TO DEVELOPING COUNTRIES

We shall now examine the practical possibilities of financing this new policy, a very important problem that is the main key to the system. Because the economic crisis affects all countries, the remedial policies must also be extended globally. Seen from this perspective, an increased demand that could stimulate large investments in the industrialized countries could come from the countries of the Third World, particularly from the poorest countries. These countries, whose GNP is now lower than $500 per capita annually, have large needs to satisfy.

In fact, if we take into consideration the extent of the natural resources not yet exploited, and the enormous reservoir of manpower available in the less developed countries, it appears certain that their development would become a factor of progress and equilibrium for the developed countries as well.

To reach this objective, steps need to be taken for the creation of an international fund disposing of sufficiently large financial resources to undertake investments in all countries, especially developing countries. The interdependence of national economies is a reality and also a determining factor for economic progress through-out the world.

Investments for industrialization of developing countries also are an imperative need because the exaggerated increase of invest-ment in the industrialized countries is engendering largescale pollu-tion and other environmental disturbances. These negative effects in the developed world make it necessary to study new criteria for a worldwide development strategy.

What should be the size of this international fund? What re-sources will be sufficient to contribute to economic growth and to satisfy the needs of the peoples in the developing countries?

According to estimates by the United Nations Secretariat, an amount of $15 to $20 billion per year over five years would suffice to create conditions favoring a sustained and continuous growth on national as well as international levels.

Is it possible to find such a sum? What conditions would be required to obtain this financing? We would answer that an annual contribution of $20 billion to this international fund is not exces-sive in size, nor is it really difficult to find. It would correspond to 0.5 percent of the GNP of the nine industrialized countries belong-ing to the Development Aid Committee of OECD. Furthermore, this figure is lower than the obligation envisaged by the United Nations in its resolutions recommending that governmental as-sistance to developing countries to equal to 0.7 percent of the GNP of the industrialized countries.

The funds, when obtained, must be equitably distributed and placed at the disposal of the developing countries on favorable conditions (interest-free, with amortization over 15 years and a grace period of 3 years) according to a procedure we shall analyze further on. Such a transfer, accomplished through the intermediary of an international agency, would make possible the attainment of a triple result: to bring about an increase of productive capacity in the undeveloped regions and of the purchasing power of their popu-lations; by augmenting purchasing power in the less developed countries, to increase their capacity to absorb imported goods and services, which could stimulate the productive capacity of the in-dustrialized countries and; to furnish the financial means necessary to accelerate the development of the less developed countries, thus making it possible for them to wipe out chronic poverty and enter the path of progressive social advance.

Thus, the transfer of a small part of the income of the rich countries could contribute to worldwide development. Let us not forget that the Marshall Plan, which had as its aim assistance to European countries suffering from the effects of World War II, also was a powerful stimulant for the recovery and the rapid development of the U.S. economy during the early postwar period. The rate of unemployment in the United States fell from 6.2 percent in 1952 to 2.2 percent in 1955—a record low in the annals of the U.S. labor market.

COST AND COVERAGE OF FINANCING: TAX OR LOAN?

The accomplishment of such financing does not appear impossible. It could take the form of a gift, which could be more equitable and more in conformity with the needs of our times; it also could take the form of an interest-free loan.

In the first case, the cost for each industrial country would be equivalent to 0.5 percent of its GNP, paid through a tax collected in favor of the countries of the Third World, especially the poorest ones. The tax would be based on the principle of international solidarity and would aim to achieve an equitable distribution of wealth on a worldwide scale. This idea, which we formulated for the first time in 1972 in *The Third World and the Rich Countries* and which was subsequently adopted by the Conference of the 77 (held in Manila, February 1976), envisages "the institution by the developed countries of a development tax which can procure for them the necessary budgetary resources without requiring that legislative bodies vote funds for this purpose each year."

In the second case, interest-free loans, the capital would be reimbursed in 15 years with a grace period of 3 years and the only charge for the developed countries would be the interest forgone at a rate of about 7 percent a year. Table 8.1 shows the gross domestic product (GDP) of the industrialized countries and the amounts equivalent to 0.5 percent of their GDP, plus annual interest at the 7 percent rate.

In either of the two alternative cases mentioned, it would be possible to obtain the sums necessary for financing the developing

TABLE 8.1

GDP of the Industrialized Countries Belonging to the OECD Development Assistance Committee, 1975

Country	GDP (in billions of $)	GDP Per Capita (in $)	0.5% of GDP (in millions of $)	Annual Interest at 7% (in millions of $)
Australia	83.3	6,245	416.5	29.1
Austria	38.2	5,063	191.0	13.4
Belgium	64.4	6,590	322.0	22.5
Canada	151.3	6,731	756.5	53.0
Denmark	35.6	7,056	178.0	12.5
Finland	26.6	5,674	133.0	9.3
France	331.4	6,313	1,657.0	116.0
Germany	429.7	6,925	2,148.5	150.4
Italy	171.9	3,105	859.5	60.2
Japan	484.6	4,417	2,423.0	169.6
Netherlands	81.5	6,017	407.5	28.5
New Zealand	13.2	4,335	66.0	4.6
Norway	28.6	7,177	143.0	10.0
Sweden	67.3	8,251	336.5	23.6
Switzerland	53.6	8,319	268.0	18.8
United Kingdom	227.0	4,049	1,135.0	79.4
United States	1,477.7	6,974	7,388.5	517.2
Total	3,765.9	5,833	18,829.5	1,318.1

Source: OECD Observer, March-April 1976.

countries through a contribution of 0.5 percent of GDP without provoking new inflationary pressures. In fact, all industrialized countries at present devote large sums to unemployment insurance payments, up to 80 or even 90 percent of previous wages. We have seen that this amounts to a total of $25 billion annually. The United States alone foresaw for 1976 an expenditure of $19 billion for unemployment insurance payments.

Furthermore, these unemployment indemnities, although socially indispensable, provoke further inflationary pressures and, as we have seen, lead through a linkage effect to more complex social problems.

In the case of the interest-free loan, the burden would not be very heavy for the industrialized countries: it would not exceed $1.3 billion. Moreover, this financing would not involve loans of money to the developing countries but rather capital goods and services. This method of financing would increase the production and the export capacity of the industrialized countries while at the same time reducing the number of unemployed, which would mean a large decrease in the expenditures devoted to unemployment payments.

We believe this idea is sound and its application would be beneficial for all countries. Active international cooperation to meet the need of all peoples, particularly those who live in poverty, may be considered an essential act of constructive wisdom, a common task for all mankind. This way of looking at the problem of development is in fact simply based on the need for worldwide social justice. When will we recognize that we all belong to the same single world community?

FOR A NEW MANAGEMENT OF INTERNATIONAL FINANCING

The proposals in this study—particularly those concerning the transfer of financial, technological, and scientific assistance through a rational use of 0.5 percent of the GDP of the industrialized countries as well as a third of the increased value of gold (see

Chapter 9)—presuppose the existence of appropriate institutions to undertake the management of this financing. The system of financing we suggest envisages a special procedure, described below.

First, a single international institution should be set up to administer the funds that each country would place at its disposal, among other things for loans to the developing countries. This institution could be the World Bank, which already has an administrative apparatus and substantial experience in evaluating the needs of the developing countries. But on one condition: that the bank be completely reorganized in order to become the "Central Financing Bank" of the Third World countries. This international institution also should coordinate the functioning of other bodies now specializing in this kind of financing, such as the IDA and IFC.

Each industrialized country should place at the disposal of the international management institution, in this case the World Bank, a sum equivalent to 0.5 percent of its GNP for the preceding year. According to available data, the global amount can be estimated at $19 billion. This amount would be placed in a special account called the "Fund for Financing the Developing Countries." As for the gold fund, the government of each developed country would transfer an amount equivalent to one third of the increased value of its gold reserves to the same special account, where it would be credited under the heading "gold." The funds thus transferred would be used by the World Bank for loans to the developing countries, without interest to those with low per capita national income or at an equitable interest rate for those with medium incomes. The amounts paid for amortization of the loans granted would be transmitted to the account of the creditor country.

The developing countries wishing to benefit from this financing would apply to the World Bank, presenting a plan for use of the loan—a plan that would be part of a national long-term plan approved by the competent national authorities. After examination of the application, the World Bank could authorize the applicant country to purchase in any country of its choice the needed capital equipment or goods.

However, it must be noted that in certain developing countries the nation's resources and foreign assistance are badly used and often wasted on purposes other than economic development.

Certainly, the preparation of the plan and of projects under the plan are the sole responsibility of the countries concerned. But when loans on favorable conditions are to be granted, the international body—provided that its operations are removed from all political influences—has the right to examine the use of the financial resources to be sure it promotes real progress. Very often governments of developing countries fail to take the radical measures and make the structural changes necessary so that their people may participate in development. Let us not forget that development implies profound mutations in economic, social, institutional, and cultural structures. The interested governments must undertake reforms, or they may face troubles that can endanger national unity.[1]

After the approval of the loan by the World Bank, the beneficiary government would be able to apply to one or several countries to purchase the needed goods or services. That is, the government would be free to purchase from any industrial enterprise the technology or products selected, up to the total amount of the approved sum.

The contracting enterprises that supply goods or services, after obtaining authorization from the governments of the industrialized and developing countries concerned, would receive payments from the "Fund for Financing the Developing Countries."

This method of financing is designed to benefit the economies of the developing countries and the industrialized countries as well.

ALLEVIATION OF OLD DEBTS

One necessary condition for the stimulation and acceleration of the development of the Third World is a cleansing of the present financial situation. This also would provide them with significant

---

1. Angelos Angelopoulos, *The Third World and the Rich Countries* (New York: Praeger, 1974).

supplementary financing resources, for their financial situation has become untenable as a result of their heavy debt service payments. Let us first see the financial situation for the developing countries.

According to the World Bank, the nonamortized external debt of the 86 developing countries amounted to $118.8 billion as of December 31, 1973, made up as follows:

	in billions of dollars
Public debt (of the state or guaranteed by the state)	56.3
Multilateral loans and credits	24.0
Suppliers' credits	12.8
Banks	17.8
Various	7.9
Total	118.8

Since 1973 this debt has increased enormously. The external deficit provoked by price increases for oil and imported industrial products has sharply accelerated the indebtedness of the Third World countries. It is estimated that the increase has been on the order of $40 billion in two years as a result of the growing external deficits for these countries, which rose to $25 billion in 1974 and $35 billion in 1975, as compared with only $9 billion in 1973. Thus, on January 1, 1976, the external debt was on the order of $150 billion.

Furthermore, the less developed countries pay the creditor countries large sums each year in debt service. This servicing, which comprises capital amortization and interest payments, amounted to $11 billion in 1973. During that same year, the developing countries received $23,7 billion, which means that the net transfer less debt servicing amounted to $12.7 billion.[2] In other words, debt servicing absorbed 48 percent or almost half of the amounts transferred by the lenders.

---

2. See International Bank for Reconstruction and Development, *World Bank Annual Report* (Washington, D.C., 1975), p. 121.

This burden weighs heavily not only on the budgets of the indebted countries but also on their payments balances. For some countries debt service is so large it absorbs a fifth of total export receipts. Thus, in 1973 debt service was equivalent to the following percentages of exports of goods and services:[3]

Egypt	34.6	Argentina	18.3
Peru	32.5	Brazil	14.0
Uruguay	30.1	Algeria	11.3
Zambia	28.0	Turkey	10.4
Mexico	25.2	Greece	9.7
Israel	20.8	Yugoslavia	6.9
India	20.1	Spain	3.6

But this is not all. To the amount of public debt servicing must be added transfers effectuated under the heading "profits and interest" on private investments. For 1969 this sum amounted to approximately $6.3 billion, as compared with $5.2 billion for public debt servicing. Thus, for 1969 the total amount required for servicing foreign capital equaled 70 percent of the total amount of fresh capital received.[4]

Since 1969 the situation has continued to deteriorate and it will shortly become untenable. Alleviation of the burden of old debts as well as new financing of the kind we are suggesting, are two problems that must be faced simultaneously and without delay.

The conditions for alleviation should be simple, uniform, and generous. The alleviation should extend to all public debts or debts guaranteed by the state, including loans granted by international organizations like the World Bank, the International Monetary Fund, the IFC, and the IDA. As regards private debts, it would be useful to begin negotiations between the parties concerned to reach reasonable agreements. The various loans granted

---

3. Ibid.
4. Angelopoulos, *The Third World*.

by each country should be consolidated, under the guidance of an international body, into one or several new loans on the following conditions for the future:

Rate of interest	2 percent
Amortization period	40 years
Grace period	7 years

Such an arrangement should satisfy the two interested parties. Thanks to this alleviation, the debtor countries would benefit from an important supplementary assistance. This should enable them to avoid a crisis and provide a means of financing new investments.

Such an arrangement also would be beneficial to the creditor countries, for by helping their debtors they would obtain reassurance that the borrowed capital would be entirely repaid. On the other hand, it must be taken into account that the excessive indebtedness of the less developed countries is attributable in large part to the rich countries which, through suppliers' credits and tied aid, have often obtained prices that far exceeded those on the world market.

Let us now see what this alleviation of public debt could bring to the developing countries in the form of financial relief and economies in foreign exchange.

According to World Bank projections, payments for servicing the external public debts of the 86 developing countries would be on the order of $72.6 billion during the seven-year grace period. This servicing would be made up as follows during these seven years:

year	billions of dollars
1976	12.9
1977	12.1
1978	11.4
1979	10.5
1980	9.4
1981	8.5
1982	7.8
Total	72.6

The first consequence of this alleviation would be immediate relief for the Third World countries of $72 billion or about $10 billion per year, and a corresponding saving of foreign exchange in the same amount. This would be of major importance for their payments balances. Furthermore, these countries would obtain an important annual saving at the expiration of the grace period. For then the old debts, now consolidated, would bear an interest rate of 2 percent instead of the present 8 percent. Further relief would be provided by the very long period of amortization in 40 annual installments instead of an effective period of five to ten annual installments, as practiced today.

Thus, through the double system of financing we propose, the developing countries would obtain a total of $200 billion during these seven years. This would constitute a decisive factor for the acceleration of growth, not only in the developing countries but also in the industrialized countries—especially since the capital equipment indispensable for this growth would come in large part from the industrialized countries.

We would add that these two procedures—a new system of financing and the alleviation of existing debts—are closely linked; neither could reach its objectives without the simultaneous application of the other. For it would not suffice to improve the present situation without creating conditions favorable for future financing. More favorable financing conditions serve no purpose if the resources obtained are absorbed by a crippling debt service burden. Therefore, these two problems must be solved simultaneously.

On the other hand, it must be emphasized that this alleviation, a measure of a quite exceptional character, should be followed by the adoption of a healthy policy within each developing country, especially in the budgetary, monetary and balance-of-payments areas.

It may also be noted that the countries of Eastern Europe have felt unfavorable repercussions from the recession and the monetary crisis. To cover the deficits in their commercial balances, they have had recourse to the Euromarket during recent years. In fact, the commercial deficit of the Eastern European countries toward the six main industrialized countries of the OECD reached $6.9 billion in 1975.

The cumulative indebtedness of the planned economy countries reached an estimated sum of $31 billion at the end of 1975, that is, equivalent to 20 months of their export receipts.

According to these estimates, the most indebted countries are the USSR ($13 billion), Poland ($6 billion), and East Germany ($3.5 billion). It may be noted that about a fourth of the total debt is owed to West Germany.[5]

IMMEDIATE MEASURES IN FAVOR
OF THE POOREST COUNTRIES

When examining the problem of alleviating the debts of the developing countries, distinctions should be made with respect to the least advanced and most seriously indebted of these countries. The poorest are so overburdened by debt service that immediate alleviation is required.[6] The developing countries have proposed convening a conference of the main creditor and debtor countries under UNCTAD auspices, to determine principles for debt renegotiation.

However, none of the conferences thus far has succeeded in formulating concrete proposals. Solutions have been adjourned and further deterioration has taken place in the financial situation of the most seriously affected countries.

Certain specific measures could be taken for these countries, without creating serious financial complications for creditors:[7]

1. With respect to the least advanced countries, whose total debt amounted to $1.6 billion at the end of 1974 and whose annual debt servicing was $110 million, the annulment of the debt service may be envisaged (as also proposed by OECD). This would ease their financial situation without imposing a heavy burden on the creditors.

---

5. See *Le Monde*, August 31, 1976, article by Alain Vernhole.

6. This urgent need was again emphasized during the proceedings of the fourth UNCTAD at Nairobi in March 1976.

7. Some interesting suggestions and information on the problem of the indebtedness of the developing countries may be found in the studies pre-

2. With respect to the most seriously affected countries (excluding the least advanced countries referred to above), whose debt service comes to $600 million annually, the application of a moratorium for some years might be envisaged with respect to interest payments to countries belonging to the OECD Development Assistance Committee (DAC). This moratorium would represent important assistance to these countries. India, for example, paid $370 million in 1974 to service its debt to creditors in DAC member countries. In that same year India received from DAC member countries only a net sum of $566 million in public aid.

The application of these proposals—that is, the cessation of debt service for the least advanced countries and a moratorium for the most seriously affected countries—would mean an annual loss of $670 million in debt service receipts. If, however, these payments are postponed to a later date—a minimum measure that is necessary and urgent—the economic cost would be $70 million per year for the period of the moratorium. Table 8.2 shows the annual loss of debt service payments for public development assistance (PDA) at the 1974 level that would be incurred by the DAC countries.

These measures of alleviation are all the more necessary because otherwise, as a result of the overwhelming burden of their external debt, these countries would be inexorably led toward a grave financial and economic crisis.

The solution of this crucial problem will greatly depend on the attitude of the creditor countries. The DAC members have begun to understand the increasing importance of the problem. The DAC working group has made an interesting analysis of this subject, defining the issues and reflecting the views of its members.[8]

---

pared by the OECD Directorate for Development Cooperation. See especially the OECD report, *Total External Debts of the Developing Countries* (Paris, 1975).

8. See the study by the DAC secretariat on the problems of indebtedness of the developing countries, published in 1974 and transmitted to the UNCTAD group examining this problem.

TABLE 8.2

**Payments to DAC Member Countries in 1974 for PDA Debt
Service by the Least Advanced Countries and by Other
Seriously Affected Countries
(in millions of dollars)**

DAC Creditors	Debt Service	
	Least Advanced Countries	Other Countries Seriously Affected
Belgium	0.2	1.3
Canada	—	0.2
Denmark	0.2	0.5
France	10.2	46.6
Germany	20.5	104.4
Italy	6.2	32.8
Japan	1.1	102.5
Netherlands	0.6	8.2
Sweden	0.8	0.2
Switzerland	—	0.8
United Kingdom	13.1	82.0
United States	30.0	65.3
Total of DAC Creditors	82.9	444.8

Source: Office of Cooperation for Development, OECD, "Report on the
Foreign Debt Obligations of Developing Countries," 1973.

Certain countries, such as Sweden, the Netherlands, Norway,
and Finland, favor collective international action for the alleviation of debts. They are ready to apply a moratorium on the debt
service of the most seriously affected countries and the least advanced countries, or to participate in any other measure capable
of furnishing these countries with immediately usable foreign
exchange. Let us hope that before the situation becomes extremely

untenable the example set by these countries will be followed by the other industrial countries belonging to DAC.

According to estimates prepared by Professor W. Leontief and associates, presented in a report to the United Nations in November 1976, if present trends continue the deficits of the developing countries on current accounts will reach a total of about $190 billion (1970) by the year 2000.[9]

We should not forget the lesson of history that heavily indebted countries are obliged sooner or later to recognize their incapacity to meet their obligations—in other words, to declare themselves bankrupt. In the fifth century B.C., when the Athenian people had sunk or sank into indebtedness, the great philosopher Solon, who was called upon mediate, introduced a law ordering the abolition of old debts.

The only way of avoiding so radical a measure is to arrange in good time the reduction of the burden of old debts. The Group of 77 is already demanding such a measure. The Conference of Manila held in February 1976, at which 121 developing countries participated, demanded "annulment of the public debts of the least advanced countries, of the developing countries which are land-locked and the island countries" and that "the other countries most seriously affected should benefit from the same treatment or at least be relieved of payments for servicing their public debts."

Furthermore, it is a fact that as time passes the strength of the Third World increases in an irreversible way. During the period between the third UNCTAD of Santiago in 1972 and the fourth UNCTAD of Nairobi in 1976, these countries have reinforced their position on the basis of their majority in the United Nations. They will become more and more demanding.

---

9. See. W. Leontief and associates, *The Future of the World Economy: A Study on the Impact of Prospective Economic Issues and Policies on International Development Strategies* (New York: Oxford University Press, 1977).

9

AN INTERIM PROPOSAL: THE RECYCLING OF PETRODOLLARS AND OF THE INCREASED VALUE OF GOLD

COVERING THE DEFICITS OF THE OIL-IMPORTING COUNTRIES

The proposals we have just presented on sources of financing are intended to form a coherent policy for recovery from the present economic recession, to promote sustained growth, and to ensure continuous economic and social progress for the world as a whole. But a preparatory interval is necessary before such a policy can be adopted, that is, until the time when the United Nations is ready to take the necessary decisions and to make recommendations for the effective application of the policy indicated.

In the meantime, immediate and practical measures can be taken to help the developed and the developing countries prepare for closer international cooperation. Among these measures may be mentioned a proposal that we made in January 1975 for the recycling of the surpluses derived from the incomes of the oil-producing countries and the increase in the value of gold held by the industrialized countries.[1]

---

1. The basic elements of this proposal have been described in the international press. An extensive summary was published in the British journal *International Currency Review* (London, March-April 1975).

Our proposal was based on the joint responsibility of the OPEC countries and the industrialized countries for the functioning of the international economic system. It was favorably received by many statesmen and by the specialized press. We now present it, readjusted to most recent economic developments and to current international conditions.

The first part of this proposal concerns the surplus derived from the incomes of the OPEC countries. On the basis of our preceding analysis, it would appear that the OPEC countries will each year have an available surplus of $30 billion at least, after deducting the amounts necessary to pay for their imports. Each year this surplus follows the Euromarket road toward the industrialized countries and the developing countries. The creditor countries thus receive through this Eurodollar financing an annual revenue (calculated on the basis of the present interest rate of 5.5 percent for three-month placements) amounting to $1.1 billion on the sum of $20 billion invested.

Our proposal is that the OPEC countries place this capital in a continuous way with the International Monetary Fund (IMF), rather than through the Euromarket channel with banks that require the borrowing countries to pay commissions and other bank charges. The IMF would be the administrator of this capital, responsible to the OPEC countries that own the funds.

The IMF would utilize the fund of $20 billion to grant loans to oil-importing countries. The system would function for a period of five years under the following lending conditions:

For the industrialized countries (25 percent of the total):

Interest rate	7 percent
Amortization period	10 years
Grace period	3 years

For the developing countries (40 percent of the total):

Interest rate	5 percent
Amortization period	15 years
Grace period	3 years

For the countries whose GNP is less than $200 per capita per year (35 percent of the total):

Interest rate	3 percent
Amortization period	18 years
Grace period	5 years

This method of financing could replace and enlarge the present oil facilities of the IMF, whose conditions of lending are less favorable to borrowers than those we propose. In fact, the total lent under the oil facilities was $7.5 billion in 1975—an insufficient amount on which the interest rate was 7 percent and the amortization period seven years. Moreover, these facilities are granted only to countries whose payments deficits are increasing. Two thirds of the funds lent under these facilities went to a small group of industrialized countries and two fifths to only two of those countries—Italy and Great Britian.[2]

The effects of a financing such as we have proposed would be favorable for all countries. For the developing countries, especially the poorest ones, this assistance would be a major aid to develop-

---

2. The main loans made under the "oil facilities" for 1975 (in millions of dollars) were as follows:

Italy	1,673
Great Britain	1,150
Spain	658
India	461
Yugoslavia	327
Korea	291
Chile	280
New Zealand	275
Pakistan	272
Turkey	195
Greece	179
Israel	165
41 other countries	1,541
Total	7,477

Source: The Economist (London), March 27, 1976.

ment. On the other hand, for the industrialized countries this method of financing would facilitate economic recovery and help to reduce their payments deficits. Even countries that do not have deficits could use this financing to pay off debts contracted on less favorable conditions (higher interest rates, shorter amortization periods). In this case, it would also be beneficial if the industrialized countries used the difference from which they profit to set up a special fund for public investments at home.

Another consideration is that economic recovery in the developed countries would tend further to increase oil imports. This would have a repercussion effect benefiting the oil-producing countries. The most important result of this method of financing would be the creation of a climate of confidence, which is essential for a sustained economic revival. The existence of a capital market offering favorable conditions, under the management of an international institution, would bring into operation a psychological factor of prime importance.

The cost of the system we propose will not be great for the OPEC countries if we take into account the advantages they would derive because management of their funds would now be handled through an international institution—a management in which, moreover, they would participate. The ultimate cost may be considered as less than nothing. Under this method of financing the OPEC countries would not be obliged to use banks and the Euromarket as intermediaries and would benefit from a sure and stable income.

But let us consider the cost of the financing conditions we propose. Assuming that 25 percent of the amount of $20 billion would be absorbed by the industrialized countries, 40 percent by the developing countries, and the rest by the poorer countries, and also taking into account the differences in the interest rates and the amortization periods, we reach the conclusion that the annual cost for the OPEC countries during the whole amortization period would average $110 million. This cost would apparently correspond to 0.1 percent of their annual oil revenues, calculated on the basis of present market prices for oil. In other words, the total cost of this system to the OPEC countries over five years would amount to

$10 billion, that is to 2 percent of their oil income for this period.[3] The management of this financing would be the same as already described for the transfer of 0.5 percent of the GNP of the industrialized countries for the benefit of the developing countries.

USING THE INCREASED VALUE OF GOLD

The second part of the recycling operation would be to use one third of the increased value of gold to provide finance on favorable conditions for the poorest developing countries. We already have elaborated this proposal, first in a memorandum to the president of the World Bank, Robert McNamara, in December 1969, and then in two books.[4] Our proposal is based on the fact that the increase in the value of gold represents a patrimony belonging to mankind as a whole. It is not permissible that this wealth should become entirely the property of the central banks, which acquired their gold reserves at a much lower price than that which would have prevailed if market conditions had been the same as for all other goods.

Social justice demands an equitable distribution of this increase in value. If the total of this increase—which at a price of $130 per ounce would amount to $108 billion—were to revert to the rich countries this would shock public opinion, particularly in the Third World. We believe at least a third of this increase in value should be used for the development of the poor countries.

In reality this contribution would be equivalent to a tax on the increased value of gold in favor of the poorest countries, in accord with the principle of international solidarity. As already explained, this tax would be fully justified. In all countries, benefits derived from an "automatic" increase in value—such as the increased value

---

3. This amount includes the total servicing of the loan throughout its duration, as provided in the agreements proposed.

4. Angelos Angelopoulos, *Gold in the Service of the Developing Countries* (Geneva: Nagel, 1970) and *The Third World and the Rich Countries* (New York: Praeger, 1973).

of land arising from a strong demand for housing or from public works—are heavily taxed by the state because they are derived from measures of general economic and social improvement and cannot be attributed to the owner's individual effort.

Should not the same be done in the case of the increased value resulting from a readjustment in the price of gold, a price long maintained unchanged by international agreement? There is no doubt that this should be done. In the case of gold, it is the state itself that profits from an unearned benefit whose creation is not due to internal and national causes but to international factors. In this case, what body should be empowered on the international level to tax a part of this profit?

The United Nations undoubtedly is the most competent body to exercise this supranational taxation role. All developing countries should ask the United Nations to adopt a resolution requiring that, in the event any reevaluation of gold takes place, one third of the increased value automatically should be transferred to the World Bank to finance the poorest countries.

Assuming a $130 per ounce price, the total increase in value would be $108 billion, as already indicated. A third of this increased value, or $36 billion, represents an amount sufficient to finance the poorest of the developing countries on favorable terms for five years.

This sum of about $36 billion could be increased if the Eastern European countries, especially the Soviet Union, agreed to participate in this system of distribution. We believe that these countries would have every interest in participating, as otherwise developing countries would rely upon the nonsocialist industrialized countries because of the favorable financing conditions they offer. If the Soviet Union, whose gold reserves can be estimated at $14 billion, were to participate, a supplementary amount of $13 billion would be added to the sum of $36 billion, thus constituting a "Fund for Financing the Poor Countries" totaling about $50 billion.

Table 9.1 shows the increase in the value of gold reserves by country or groups of countries and as a total for all countries.

We have always argued that the financing supplied through the transfer of one third of the increased value of gold should be

TABLE 9.1

Distribution of Gold Reserves, 1975
(millions of dollars)

Country	Value at $35 Per Ounce	Value at $130 Per Ounce	Difference
United States	9,280	34,648	25,368
United Kingdom	723	2,699	1,976
Canada	742	2,770	2,028
West Germany	3,973	14,832	10,859
Belgium	1,424	5,318	3,894
Denmark	61	229	168
France	3,410	12,731	9,321
Italy	2,786	10,403	7,617
Netherlands	1,835	6,850	5,015
Norway	33	124	91
Sweden	196	730	534
Switzerland	2,810	10,493	7,683
Austria	705	2,634	1,929
Other European countries	1,772	6,615	4,843
Australia	249	929	680
South Africa	610	2,278	1,668
Oil-producing countries	1,191	4,448	3,257
Other Western countries	596	2,225	1,629
Other Middle East countries	500	1,866	1,366
Other countries	661	2,470	1,809
Total (all countries)	34,270	127,954	93,684
International bodies	5,183	19,351	14,168
Grand Total	39,453	147,305	107,853

granted in accord with the procedure described in Chapter 8. The loans would be made in the form of goods and services, and not of foreign exchange. In other words, each country holding gold should use the equivalent of a third of the increase in value to permit the purchase of goods and services by the developing countries through the intermediary of an international institution, in this case the World Bank, appropriately reorganized. Consequently, the country holding gold would not sell it on the free market in order to furnish help to the poor countries, but would use the increase in value resulting from reevaluation to pay suppliers transferring equipment to the poor countries of the Third World.

A decision analogous to our proposal was taken by the IMF in August 1975 in Washington and was further elaborated at the Jamaica Conference in January 1976. According to this decision, a trust fund will be created to supply credits on preferential conditions to the poorest countries. The fund will be fed by the sale of one sixth, or 25 million ounces, of the gold deposited with the IMF. The sales will be spread over four years.

At first sight, the two systems (that of the IMF and ours) appear roughly identical. It has even been written that the IMF decision was based on our initial proposal submitted in 1969 to the World Bank. However, there are fundamental differences between the two proposals and we want to present some clarifications on this point:

1. There is a great difference in the amount to be used to finance the poor countries. Under our proposal, which envisages use of one third of the increase in value of total gold reserves, the amount available for financing would be $36 billion as we have just seen. Under the IMF proposal this amount would only be $2.4 billion. This very large difference considerably reduces the financing fund.

2. Our proposal refers not only to the gold held by the IMF but to the totality of gold held by central banks in particular.

3. Our proposal does not envisage the sale of gold to banks or on the free market. It calls for utilization of a third of the profit from a revaluation of gold as state credits to pay suppliers of goods and services for the development of the poor countries. This procedure would facilitate a neutralization of inflationary

pressures. On the contrary, the sale of gold by the IMF creates a risk of bringing into the monetary crisis a speculative factor and an additional element of disorder.

4. For reasons we shall explain in the following chapter, the gold should remain with the central banks and the IMF as a kind of guarantee for the stability of the new monetary system we propose. The developing countries have every interest in demanding the termination of the IMF gold sales and in seeking to use the counter-value of the gold sales in another way that would not have unfavorable repercussions on the price of gold.

MONETARY POLICY AND ECONOMIC POLICY

Monetary policy must be a part of an overall economic and social policy. Its objectives must be harmonized with general policies so it can play an active role in the achievement of international economic progress.

Monetary stability presupposes economic stability. And if monetary policy can contribute to the success of economic policy, it is also true that a monetary crisis can aggravate an economic crisis. A close interdependence therefore exists between these two policies, which must constitute a coherent and coordinated whole.

This interdependence is clearly seen in developments during the years 1971-76, when monetary fluctuations reflected economic fluctuations.[1] In fact, the suspension of the official convertibility of the dollar into gold in August 1971 and the abandonment of the

---

1. Johannes Witteveen, director general of the IMF, has emphasized that "the rapid growth of trade and of capital movements during the past 20 years was reflected in the increasing integration and interdependence of national economics on the world scale." IMF *Bulletin*, June 2, 1975.

fundamental principle of the Bretton Woods system, whereby
parities were established in agreement with the IMF, marked the beginning of a transitional period characterized by a permanent crisis
that has yet to be resolved by a definitive international monetary
system.

Undoubtedly the monetary system established in 1944 at Bretton Woods did contribute during the postwar period to the recovery
and development of the economies of the Western world. In a Europe ravaged by war, the establishment of monetary order and stability—supported to a certain degree by the compensatory role of
the IMF in applying a system of fixed exchange rates with only
limited fluctuations permitted—did facilitate the growth of trade by
creating a climate of confidence and optimism. Over time, the conditions of economic life have changed decisively, both on the national and the international levels. Trade and commercial relations
have taken on very large dimensions and the relative power of various countries has undergone transformation. The initial Bretton
Woods system no longer corresponds to international requirements.

We do not wish to enter into a detailed analysis of the evolution of the monetary system, since its profound changes are widely
known and have often been analyzed by experts.[2] We shall only examine certain characteristic elements linked to the deeper causes of
the present crisis.

The system's basic characteristic has been the maintenance of
fixed parity between different currencies and the price of gold
(with a maximum rate of 1 percent fluctuation), using the dollar as
a medium of exchange for all other currencies (the gold exchange
standard system). Thus, for gold to be accepted as a standard of exchange its price had to be fixed and expressed in dollars. This

---

2. An analysis of the monetary problem is contained in *Essais en
l'Honneur de Jean Marchal*, vol. 2: *La Monnaie* (Paris: Cujas, 1975). See also
IMF, *Reform of the International Monetary System* (Washington, D.C.: 1972);
Robert Triffin, *Le Système monétaire international* (Paris, 1969); Charles
Kindleberger, *Power and Money* (London: Macmillan, 1970); J. L'Huillier,
Le Système monétaire international (Paris, 1971); P. Simonnot, *Pour une
Réforme monétaire* (Paris, 1972); X. Zolotas, *Alternative Systems for Inter-
national Monetary Reform* (Athens: Papazissis Publishers, 1965); X. Zolotas,
From Anarchy to International Monetary Order (Athens: Bank of Greece,
1973); John Kenneth Galbraith, *Money* (Boston: Houghton Mifflin, 1976).

meant that the dollar enjoyed great confidence on the international level, to such a degree that it might be asked—as was done in a study by the Economic and Social Council of France—"whether the dollar was guaranteed by gold or whether gold was guaranteed by the dollar like a raw material whose price had been stabilized."

Because of this need to maintain a fixed price for gold and the great dependence of the entire international monetary system on the stability of a single national currency, the dollar, under the influence of dynamic changes in the international economy, contributed to the creation of inflationary pressures that have led to the present crisis.

In effect, when the prices of various goods and especially industrial products increased considerably over time, the maintenance of the official gold price fixed at the conventional level of $35.2 per ounce was unrealistic. The report of the Bank for International Settlements in June 1976 stated that "The disappointments of the twelve years following [this decision] may be attributed in large part to the fundamental contradiction that existed between trying to make reforms while excluding a priori any discussion of the price of gold or of the exchange rate system."[3]

This policy could only result in subjecting gold to inflationary pressures. The role of gold became ever greater as international trade increased and created needs for additional liquidity far beyond the capacity of gold to provide. As we have pointed out in another study, if a readjustment in the price of gold had been made in good time, taking into account the new situation, speculation would have been neutralized and the functioning of the international monetary system would today be more normal.[4]

Efforts to preserve the stability of the price of gold were unsuccessful. In 1961, in order to maintain this stability, a gold pool was created, composed of the economically and financially most powerful countries of the Western world. They sought to

---

3. Bank for International Settlements, *Forty-Sixth Annual Report* (Basel, June 1976), p. 129.

4. See Angelos Angelopoulos, *Gold in the Service of Developing Countries* (Geneva: Nagel, 1969).

intervene in the market, sometimes as seller and sometimes as buyer, whenever the gold price differed from the parity of $35.2 per ounce. Nevertheless, the inflationary pressures became so strong that in 1968 it was necessary to accept officially a double gold market with a differentiation between "monetary gold" maintained at a stable price and "commercial gold," whose price was determined on the free market.

Following this differentiation, the price of commercial gold rapidly increased: from $50 per ounce at the beginning of 1972 it rose to $125 by the middle of 1973; by the end of 1974 it reached the astonishing level of $200 per ounce. On the other hand, the official price of monetary gold was fixed at $42 per ounce. The official reevaluation of monetary gold in 1971 was unable to match the price of gold prevailing on the free market; naturally, for this reason it was unable to resolve the problem of equilibrium between the high prices of various goods and the price of gold.

From a purely monetary viewpoint, the reevaluation of the gold price was simply an indirect devaluation of the U.S. dollar, one of the hardest world currencies. In fact, to the problem of the insufficiency of reserves resulting from the growing scarcity of monetary gold was added the inability of the United States to adjust its foreign accounts balance. The U.S. balance of payments in 1973 registered a deficit for the first time in history—$10.7 billion—and this resulted in a dizzy spiral in dollar reserves leading U.S. authorities to suspend the convertibility of their currency in August 1971. The creation of SDRs (Special Drawing Rights) in 1969—a creation of a rather hybrid nature—came at a time when global reserves were growing with unprecedented speed. Thus, foreign exchange reserves, under the impact of the enormous swelling of the U.S. payments deficit, increased during 1970 and 1971 by $49 billion, a figure equal to more than 60 percent of total monetary reserves in the world at the end of 1969.[5]

Very large speculative movements of U.S. capital toward Europe and Japan, in addition to the exodus of dollars to cover

---

5. Bank for International Settlements, *Forty-Sixth Annual Report*, p. 129.

the international debts of the United States, contributed to the creation of an inflationary tide and decisively shattered the dollar's value. Again it is seen that monetary stability depends above all on the economic progress of each country and that a close interdependence exists between rates of exchange and inflation.

REFORMS IN THE INTERNATIONAL MONETARY SYSTEM

After the end of 1963, official discussions were begun between the ministers of finance of the Group of 10 and then in the Committee of 20 to study "the measures necessary or desirable for improvement or reform of the international monetary system." The Committee of 20, which began its work at the OECD's Chateau de la Muette near Paris only in March 1973, declared that "in the new system the exchange rate regime should remain based on stable but flexible parities," while adding that "floating rates could, however, constitute a useful procedure in particular situations."

However, the spectacular increase in the price of oil completely overturned the committee proposal envisaging creation of a new system of parities, and floating rates were maintained indefinitely. In fact, in the industrialized countries that were financially and economically strong, new conditions arose requiring changes in their monetary parities; this led to a regime of floating international parities beginning in March 1973.

Since that time the essential characteristic of the Bretton Woods system—stability in parities—no longer exists in practice, despite the maintenance by the IMF of the system's official status. As pointed out in a study submitted to the Economic and Social Council of France:

parities are now only theoretical indexes since rates of exchange can float without constraint on one side or another of par. And these theoretical indexes are expressed in a fictitious gold content, so fictitious that the double gold market was officially suppressed in November 1973. The tendency now is to express parities in special drawing rights (SDRs). But the SDRs are themselves defined by their parity—one thirty-fifth of an ounce of fictitious gold—a parity that has remained unchanged since it was originally established. Since July 1974, the SDRs have been linked to a basket of currencies; which is to say very simply that through SDRs currencies are linked to each other. In fact, at present, the value of currencies is proclaimed; it is not defined.

It is certainly true that the introduction of this regime of floating currencies was necessary and inevitable to overcome the serious difficulties encountered in international trade. Undoubtedly, in the short term the economically advanced countries have benefited from this move, which was only transitional and was to lead sooner or later to a search for a better, more stable monetary system.[6]

The recent monetary crisis in Europe, which arose during the spring of 1976 with the devaluation of sterling, the Italian lire, and later the French franc—and led to the departure of the franc from the "snake"[7]—has been termed the most serious mone-

----

6. According to X. Zolotas (see his address to the thirtieth annual assembly of the Board of Governors of the IMF, Washington, D.C., September 1-5, 1975), "a return to fixed parities could not be considered as a solution at least for the present. A free floating would not be a solution either." He added, "only an appropriately administered floating system combined with the pursuit of a monetary and anti-cyclical policy sufficiently coordinated among the main industrialized countries, could reestablish a relative stability in exchange rates." On the other hand, René Larre, director general of the Bank for International Settlements, emphasizes in his report of June 1976 that "the world will have to live with floating currencies during a rather long time ahead. This should not mean nevertheless that stability in exchange rates is an unimportant objective" (p. 154).

7. The system of the "European monetary snake" was created in April 1972 with the aim of limiting the degree of fluctuation of the currencies of the participating countries to 1.125 percent in each direction. Thus the monetary snake could move in relation to the dollar, as in a tunnel, within a fixed margin of more or less 2.25 percent. Each country was supposed to intervene on the foreign exchange market to maintain its currency within these limits. A short time afterward, Great Britain (June 1972) and Italy (February 1973) left the

tary crisis of the postwar period; it demonstrates how closely the various currencies are linked with economic problems.

Neither the Jamaica agreement—which pretended to be a very important reform of the monetary system—nor any other bilateral or multilateral agreements have succeeded in maintaining monetary stability. The lack of alignment between the economic policies of the industrialized countries and the ineffectiveness of the measures taken to combat inflation and unemployment are the root causes of the recent monetary storm. Furthermore, the rates of inflation registered in different countries have given a shock to foreign exchange rates.

As a result, Europe is divided into two monetary groups:

1. A powerful group including the Deutschemark, the Dutch florin, the Swiss franc, and the Norwegian kronor, that is, the currencies of countries where the increase in inflation is small.

2. A weak group including the currencies of countries whose inflation rates exceed 10 percent.

Under these conditions it is impossible to maintain the snake system in its present form. Either a widening of the limits of the permissible fluctuations or an abolition of the system must be foreseen.

Already a danger is arising: the reactivation of inflation and a halt to the weak economic recovery that began early in 1976. Furthermore, the meeting of the European Council of Ministers held in Luxembourg on April 2-3, 1976, recognized once more the failure of economic and monetary policies. Thus, the Nine acknowledged that it was impossible for them—as *Le Monde* wrote on April 3, 1976—"to revive their cooperation. . . . They were

---

tunnel. After the second devaluation of the dollar, the other European countries (Germany, Belgium, Denmark, France, Luxembourg, Netherlands, in association with Norway and Sweden) maintained the links between their currencies but broke off their link with the dollar and other currencies. Since the departure of France from the tunnel (March 1976), the system of the monetary snake now includes only the currencies of Germany, Belgium, the Netherlands, and Denmark as well as the associated currencies of Norway and Sweden.

satisfied to draw attention to the need not to place in question what remains of the Community."

If we look back upon the long road taken in efforts to achieve monetary reform, we conclude that these efforts have ended in failure. The use of the dollar as a currency for monetary reserves, for support, and for settlements has not been limited; nor has gold been replaced in the international monetary system by another reserve instrument. Nor, finally, has a new code of conduct been established for a system in which fixed and flexible exchange rates would move together in synchronization.[8]

Moreover, as the Bank for International Settlements has pointed out, "the present system is more complex than is generally admitted."[9] The prevailing regime is an ensemble of exchange rates for currencies linked in different ways. Thus, today 53 currencies are attached to the U.S. dollar, thirteen to the French franc, and five to the pound sterling. Moreover, six European currencies are part of the floating bloc with respect to the dollar which maintains a margin of 2.25 percent for each currency in relation to the others. Also, twelve IMF members express the rate of exchange for their currencies in terms of SDRs. Would anyone claim that such a confusing system could contribute to the solution of the present monetary crisis?

FOR A SUPRANATIONAL CURRENCY

As already explained, the reinvigoration of international economic activity through large-scale and productive investments not only would facilitate the reform of the monetary system but would constitute a primary condition for such a reform. This

8. A very interesting analysis of the evolution of the objectives of monetary reform may be found in a speech by Guido Carli, former governor of the Bank of Italy, delivered on June 12, 1976 at the thirteenth conference of the Per Jacobsson Foundation. On the same subject, see also the comments of Milton Gilbert on the dollar and the SDRs in IMF *Bulletin*, July 26, 1976.

9. Bank for International Settlements, *Forty-Sixth Annual Report.*

means that the monetary problem must be seen in the framework of long-term policy encompassing the world economy as a whole, including the economies of the socialist countries and the developing countries, whether or not they are oil producers.

If the international monetary system is to perform its role, it must be based on a supranational currency to which national currencies would be adjusted at fixed parities. What could serve as such a supranational currency? The dollar?

The dollar has ceased to be the dominant currency and SDRs are now considered neither as a reserve currency nor as an instrument for international payments. We therefore must look for a universal currency that can take a place alongside the existing monetary polycentrism—a currency that will be acceptable to all countries, including the socialist countries.

Because it is necessary to avoid the creation of new types of currency, Special Drawing Rights could be made this international currency under the following conditions:

1. That the SDRs become the main reserve currency; they may be given a short name acceptable to all, such as the obole or the cratir (the currencies of ancient Greece) or simply the "IMF dollar."

2. That this new currency, whose issuance would be controlled by the IMF, should be accepted not only as an instrument of settlement between central banks as is now the case, but especially as a means of payment in private transactions on the same terms as other currencies.

3. The issuance of the new currency must be regularized, based on the world's economic needs. The SDRs at present issued would be replaced by the new currency and a certain quantity of this new currency would be transferred to the central banks in pro rata amounts according to their holdings in gold, as we shall explain later. An additional sum should be placed at the disposal of the countries of the Third World, especially the poorest countries. On the basis of appropriate procedures, countries may buy this new supranational currency with their national

currencies while readjusting the parity of their currencies in relation to the supranational currency.

Thus, this new currency would become the supranational
reserve currency. In this way, the domination of the world market by the currency of a single country or group of countries
would be avoided; no country or group of countries would be able
in the final analysis to control the volume or the use of this currency, as is now the case with dollars.

It is indispensable for the success of this plan that the International Monetary Fund be reorganized to become a truly international institution. If this body is to function effectively, the
representation of the member countries must be as wide as possible and it must be governed in conformity with the interests
of the entire world economy. The participation of the socialist
countries should be ensured on the basis of equitable criteria. The
size of a country's GNP and population should be the two main
criteria for the quota accorded to each participating country.

In this way the IMF could become a universal institution and
be considered a body representing the world's economic potential. A fusion may even be envisaged between the International
Monetary Fund and the World Bank so that, merged into a single
institution, more rational coordination and more effective management might be obtained.

GOLD AS A MONETARY UMBRELLA FOR
THE NEW SUPRANATIONAL CURRENCY

But if a currency is to maintain its stability over the long
term, it must be linked to a standard that inspires the confidence
of other currencies. What should this standard be? Can national
income, the volume of money in circulation, gold, or some other
index create a climate of confidence assuring the stability of the
international monetary system?

Whether we like it or not, gold will long continue to play a
predominant role in international monetary policy and on the

world market; its price will continue to be a barometer of the economic and political difficulties of each country and of the world as a whole.

Of course, nobody today can favor a return to the convertibility of currencies into gold, a convertibility long ago abandoned. Even the Bretton Woods agreements sharply departed from the strict tule of complete convertibility of gold certificates. This convertibility was practiced only between governments and with important limitations. It is true that gold has for a long time been undergoing "demonetization."

However, this relative convertibility protected the monetary stability of the dollar, in a latent manner, until August 1971, when convertibility was suspended. Should we provide, with respect to the new currency we propose, a "relative convertibility" from which the dollar would benefit? This is not possible for several reasons. The United States, which produces 40 percent of the national income of the Western countries, does not wish such convertibility and U.S. gold reserves do not permit its application.

In our opinion, recourse may be had to a "plastic convertibility" using gold as a "monetary umbrella." This is how it would work:[10]

1. The gold at present held in the central banks would be frozen, under the control of the IMF. This gold stock, whose value is about $110 billion, would not in any event be used in interstate transactions. No central bank would have the right to buy or sell gold. The totality of these gold reserves would constitute a kind of coverage for the new international currency. These reserves would thus serve as a monetary umbrella in the new international system.

---

10. This idea was developed in an article published by the author in *Le Monde* of August 21, 1973 under the title "Can Gold Be Used as a Monetary Umbrella?" Later, it was presented in a report to a meeting of a group of experts held in Athens in October 1975, organized by the Geneva Research Centre for the Study of International Institutions.

2. The official price of monetary gold should be fixed. The gold-producing countries, particularly South Africa and the Soviet Union, should accept the obligation to sell each year a part of their production—for example, a fourth—to the IMF at the new official price, which would be fixed at a level close to the free market price.

3. The new officially fixed gold price would benefit from the protection on the free market of a special pool designed to ensure the stability of the gold price over a relatively long time.

4. A part of the increased value of gold—a third, as proposed in the preceding chapter—would be used to provide financing on favorable terms for the poorest countries of the Third World, through the intermediary of the World Bank. The gold would not be sold. Only the counter-value of a third of the gold held by the industrialized countries would be used to pay domestic enterprises for the supply of goods and services needed for the development of the poor countries.

5. Each country would receive from the IMF a quantity of the new international currency corresponding pro rata to its gold holdings. Also, each country would be able to buy an amount of the new currency, paying in its national currency, in accord with appropriate procedures.

The success of this system is closely linked with the world gold market, a subject we shall next examine.

THE FUTURE OF GOLD

The system of "plasmatic gold convertibility" that we have just proposed will depend above all on the role to be played by gold in monetary and economic policy during the coming years.

As is known, the price of gold has undergone large fluctuations, at first in an upward direction after 1972, reaching $200 an ounce toward the end of 1974, and then in a downward direction, dropping to $110 an ounce in August 1976. Figure 10.1 shows these fluctuations during recent years.

FIGURE 10.1

Market Prices for Gold

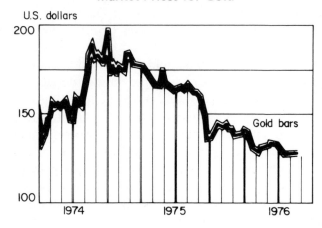

If no steps were taken to stabilize the price of gold, fluctuations would continue during the coming years as a result of certain factors that stimulate speculation, some on the offer side and some on the demand side. Let us briefly examine the most important of these factors.

First, let us look at the offer side. The production of gold shows a decline since 1970 and its cost has increased over time. In fact, production dropped from 1,267 metric tons in 1970 to 927 tons in 1975, omitting the production of the socialist countries. On the other hand, the average gold content of the ore processed has dropped by 30 percent since 1971, while average minehead export costs per ton of ore treated have more than doubled as a result of a fourfold increase in wages. [11]

The offer of gold for sale could increase, first, as a result of sales by the Soviet Union and other Eastern countries, and second

---

11. According to the *Degussa Report* (Frankfurt), published by one of the three main enterprises in the world dealing in and processing precious metals, the amount of gold sold by the Soviet Union during the first half of 1976 was 150 tons and further Soviet gold sales of 100 to 200 tons were foreseen for the remainder of the year. Also see M. Zombanakis, *Petrodollars in 1976* (London: First Boston Company, 1975).

by auction sales by the International Monetary Fund. According to estimates by Swiss banks, the sales of the Soviet Union will be on the order of 250 tons annually during the coming years.

As regards the IMF sales, the agreements reached in August 1975 during the meeting of the IMF Committee of Governors foresaw that the official gold price would be abolished, that the global gold stock of the IMF and the countries of the Group of 10 would not be increased, that one sixth of the gold reserves of the IMF would be restituted to the member countries, and that another sixth would be sold for the benefit of the developing countries. According to the decision adopted in January 1976 in Jamaica, the IMF is to auction every six weeks 780,000 ounces of gold; the first of these sales was held on June 2 and the second on July 14, 1976. As a result of this decision, 194 metric tons annually will be offered, supplementing other sources during 1977, 1978, and 1979.

Thus, the global offer during the 1977–80 period will be approximately as follows:

	tons
Production of the Western countries	900
Sales by Eastern countries	250
IMF actions	200
Total	1,350

The amount offered might be increased if South Africa were obliged to sell a part of its gold reserves, as it did recently to meet a deficit in its balance of payments. It is estimated that a lowering of the price by $10 an ounce would result in an annual loss of foreign exchange for South Africa of $220 million. Moreover, the gold production of South Africa might be reduced as a result of racial and economic conflicts, which have recently taken on alarming dimensions.

Now let us look at the demand side. During 1973 and 1974 the gold market was characterized by tremendous hoarding and investment, but in 1975, on the contrary, industrial demand predominated. It is estimated that industrial demand, which at present makes up 85 percent of total demand, will increase during coming years and will be approximately 1,300 or 1,350 tons, which would take up almost all the supply. For this reason it may be said that the market for gold will be in balance, and that large price fluctuations would not be justified.

Is the January 1977 price of gold, about $130 per ounce, a correct price that corresponds to the balance between supply and demand?

If the price of gold were to follow the price of oil, it should oscillate around $200 an ounce. But gold differs from oil with respect to its price formation. The main producers, like South Africa and the Soviet Union, do not make up a common front. On the other hand, the supply and the demand for the yellow metal are less certain. There are gold reserves, the largest part of which belong to the central banks, remain frozen, and consequently do not influence the market. But a large portion also belongs to private banks and to individuals who speculate on the gold market, and their behavior determines the price. Moreover, the gold sales policy of the IMF has sown confusion in the international market and has had unfavorable effects.

As a result of the drop in gold prices, the poor countries will receive a reduced amount of aid from the IMF. In fact, if the price of $110 an ounce is maintained, in future auction sales the poor countries will suffer a substantial loss which is of great importance due to their very unfavorable economic and financial situation.

Another unsatisfactory feature of the IMF decision is the distribution at the end of 1976 of 25 million ounces of gold to the central banks in four annual installments at the official price of about $42 an ounce. This is scandalous favoritism toward the rich countries. It is probable that these governments will be able to sell a part or all of this gold on the private market in order to acquire foreign exchange for making their international payments.

The president of the U.S. Federal Reserve Board, Arthur Burns, finds that the fall in the price of gold is "generally welcomed" because this would have a "good" influence on "international liquidity."[12] But the chairman of the Committee on International Economic Affairs of the U.S. Congress, Henry S. Reuss, takes a contrary view and disapproves of the sale of this gold. "The agreement is unfair," he has declared, "for the restitution of a part of the gold to the Central Banks will give an opportunity to the rich countries to make substantial profits while the poor developing countries will receive only meager benefits."[13]

However, the price of $126 an ounce accepted by the IMF at the first auction sale of 780,000 ounces was considered as a lower limit of an "unofficial nature, below which the metal should not fall for any long period."[14] In fact, the central banks and the governments of the developing countries have every interest in the maintenance of a high gold price. The second IMF sale of July 14, 1976, was made at the price of $122 an ounce, that is, slightly lower than the price at the first sale.

Although a further drop in gold prices cannot be excluded as a result of the atmosphere of confusion and suspicion that prevails in respect to this metal, in the long term a rise in price should be expected—a rise probably to about $150 an ounce in the coming years—on condition that the decision adopted at Jamaica is changed. Undoubtedly, the holding of 15 auctions every six weeks or so until the end of 1980 with 780,000 ounces sold each time can only feed speculation, which is detrimental to the interests of the poor countries and maintains a climate of instability.

For this reason, the IMF decision to sell gold is, as already noted, an error that must be corrected. The IMF has the right, according to the Jamaica decision, to limit or to postpone the auctions if the sales greatly influence the price of gold on the market. However, if the IMF intends to continue the auctions, the Third World countries should demand a halt to these sales, to safeguard their interests.

---

12. *International Herald Tribune* (Paris), July 13, 1976.

13. U.S. House of Representatives, September 17, 1975.

14. This view was expressed by a large Swiss bank. See *Bulletin of the Union Bank of Switzerland*, July 1976.

If effective measures, especially of an economic nature, are not adopted to put an end to monetary instability, gold will continue to prevent the smooth functioning of the international monetary system. Let us not forget that for certain countries—such as those of the Middle East, Latin America, and some countries of Europe (Italy, Portugal, and even France)—gold still constitutes an investment reserve. In these countries, when the inflation rate is high and the political situation unstable, the demand for gold does not stop. This situation is all the more likely to arise because the world economy contains a great inflationary potential—a potential that is not only monetary but also "psychological." Inflation is considered the disease of this century and each person tries to place in solid investment whatever fortune he may have. Gold, although it pays no interest, remains the symbol of security.

Thus, the price of gold reflects the economic and political difficulties of each country. For this reason, we think that a "plasmatic convertibility" based on gold—under the conditions we have suggested—can be the beginning of a stabilization of the world economy, the foundation for monetary stability, and the guarantee of worldwide economic and social progress.

We have presented these thoughts in the hope that they can contribute to the search for an international monetary system capable of facilitating trade among all the countries. The world's economic equilibrium, the revival of economic activity, and the reform of the monetary system can only be the result of a concerted effort and a common accord among all countries. Economic and social progress can be brought about solely through close and sincere international cooperation. The great industrial powers—headed by the United States, the Soviet Union, the European Economic Community, and Japan—should take the initiative of convening an international monetary conference to promote the adoption of an economic and monetary system that is equitable and effective.

At the present time, in spite of the efforts initiated by the economic and monetary authorities of various countries and by certain international organizations, the economic crisis continues and prospects for recovery remain uncertain and precarious. Recent OECD forecasts for 1977 show a rather dark picture. Unemployment is expected to persist or to increase; some 15 million workers will be without jobs. Inflation will remain at high levels in most countries. The investment rate will continue to be sluggish and slow. In the final analysis, this situation—characterized by the paradox of co-existing inflation and unemployment which has been termed "stagflation"—will also lead to a ruinous competition between the industrialized countries as they struggle to conquer markets of insufficient dimensions.

HOW TO OVERCOME THE PRESENT IMPASSE?

In my opinion, the only way out of inflation and unemployment is to adopt a new international strategy based on a recycling of funds between the industrialized and the developing countries [a plan for which is outlined in this volume].

The main element in this recycling would be the use of a very small percentage of the industrialized countries' Gross National Product—0.5 percent a year, or about 20 billion dollars—to finance productive investments in the developing countries, especially in the poorest of them, through loans by the World Bank. The developing countries would use these loans to purchase capital equipment in the industrialized "lending" countries. The loans would be

---

This appendix was published in *Le Monde*, April 14, 1977.

paid off in 15 years; there would be an interest-free grace period of five years, and the interest paid during the subsequent ten years would be five percent each year.

In this way, the only charge to the industrialized countries would be interest on the loans during the first five years, that is, $1,400 million per year and $600 million per year for the next ten-year period, for which the rate of interest would be five instead of seven percent, which is the current normal rate in the market.

The Consolidation of Existing Debts

One complementary measure which would effectively help support the plan's application and which should be undertaken simultaneously would be the consolidation of the debts owed by those developing countries participating in the financial recycling plan. It costs $13 billion annually to service these debts which now amount to some $150 billion. This $13 billion absorbs 48 percent of the amounts granted under the heading of "aid" and represents an intolerably heavy burden on the countries of the Third World. For this reason these debts should now be consolidated and amortized on favorable conditions with a five-year grace period. However, the developing countries should use the amount of debt-servicing payments thus economized exclusively for imports of equipment from countries to which such servicing amounts should be paid. This would be a fundamental requirement for any such debt consolidation and relief.

Thus, the economies of the industrialized countries would be stimulated in two ways, both by the use of the fund established to help the developing countries and by the additional purchases to be made on the basis of the debt-servicing savings from which the developing countries had benefited.

The "Multiplier" Effects

Such a plan would stimulate economic growth and social welfare in the industrialized countries while creating new purchasing power in the developing countries by giving them the means of importing additional goods and services.

It is very important to bear in mind the multiplier effects of such investments on the countries participating in the proposed Plan. The OECD has estimated such multiplier effects in a developed country as being on the order of 1.75 and, in a developing country, higher than 2.5. Hence, by stimulating the growth of the production apparatus, the total economic effects of the Plan would be much greater than the cost of initiating it. This generalized economic recovery would make possible the creation of additional national income and new fiscal resources, thus covering the financial costs during the first five years many times over.

THE "CARTER PLAN": IS A "REGIONAL PLAN" POSSIBLE?

The application of this policy presupposes a common will on the part of the industrialized countries to effect a "global plan" linking all industrialized and all developing countries. This could be the target of the Summit Conference, which is to take place in London in the beginning of May, 1977. However, if it appears that such a global plan is not at present realizable, could not a "regional plan" serve as a first step, a precursor, towards the later application of the policy we propose? We believe that a "regional plan" launched by a single industrialized country—for example, the United States of America, the greatest economic power of the world—with a group of some developing countries could be both immediately realizable and beneficial.

In order to stimulate its economic recovery and overcome an unemployment which has taken on disturbing dimensions, the United States needs a large-scale increase in productive investments. But because industrialists hesitate to make such new investments due to market uncertainties—a phenomenon which is, in fact, worldwide—a way must be found to ensure the consumption of the new products by an effective demand for expanded production through strong and permanent exports. This could be done by creating an additional effective demand for these exports in the developing countries.

Sources of Financing

How could this be accomplished?

Two questions may be raised: what is the amount of investment needed to stimulate the U.S. economy, and what method would be used to obtain the necessary funds for this financing?

First, as to the amount. We think that an additional investment of $15 billion annually over five years would be sufficient to strengthen the recovery of the U.S. economy. This sum, about one percent of the U.S. GNP, would be used for the purchase in the United States of capital equipment needed for the development of those developing countries which had decided to participate in the Plan. Such countries would submit their specific investment projects to an agency established under the authority of the Department of State, Treasury, or Commerce. The projects proposed would form an integral part of the developing countries' overall economic plans.

This Plan of financing must be in effect for a period of five years, during which time the loan would be granted free of interest and would be repaid in 15 years, the first installment of which would start in the sixth year. In this way the only burden on the United States' budget would be the amount of interest during the first five years, that is, $1 billion per year. For the following ten-year period, for which the interest would be five percent instead of seven percent, which is the current normal rate in the market, the burden on the budget would amount to $300 million yearly.

Such a financing would not create any difficulties for the United States. As a result of the economic recovery that should result, the United States would benefit from a drop in unemployment, and this would have positive effects on the national budget as well as on the economy as a whole. In fact, the creation of new jobs through such investments would bring about a progressive reduction in unemployment compensation benefits which at present cost about $17 billion each year. The sum saved on this account could cover a large part of the Plan's financing cost. Furthermore, the use of this sum for productive purposes rather than for purposes which create inflationary pressures, as is now the case with unemployment compensation payments, would have favorable economic and social effects.

A Supplementary Demand

As stated previously, the demand for new exports from the United States would be completed by the utilization of an amount of about $7 billion yearly, which represents the servicing of loans owed by developing countries to the United States. The amount so economized by the developing countries through the postponement during the first five years of debt-servicing payments would be used to place new orders for U.S. goods and services for their productive investments.

In this way, the U.S. economy would be further stimulated for steady expansion, as was the case under the Marshall Plan. It may be recalled that the application of the Marshall Plan made it possible to reduce unemployment in the United States within three years—from 6.2 percent in 1952 to 2.2 percent in 1955.

I strongly believe that President Carter, who in his inaugural address and in his message to foreign countries expressed in an admirable and convincing way his aim to abolish injustice and the scourges of poverty, hunger, illness, and political repression, would be able to take the initiative to adopt such a policy as it fits in perfectly with his philosophy of building a new world order reflecting the aspirations of humanity as a whole.

ANGELOS ANGELOPOULOS, member of the Academy of Athens, Governor of the National Bank of Greece, and formerly a professor at the University of Athens, is an economist known both in Greece and internationally for his scientific activities and numerous works on economic and social questions. For a number of years he was Director of the Economic Council of Greece, and later he founded and presided over the Greek Economic Planning Association, which formulated the bases for Greece's first five-year plan.

Professor Angelopoulos is a member of a number of international institutes concerned with political economy, public finance, statistics, and demographic questions. He is a frequent contributor to several leading journals and newspapers, and he lectures at various universities.

Among his more recent publications are *Planisme et progres social, Will the Atom Unite the World?* (this book, in which he examines the economic aspects of atomic energy, has been translated into 12 languages), *Theory and Policy of Economic Development* (in Greek), *The Third World and the Rich Countries* (translated into 11 languages).

In 1967 Professor Angelopoulos resigned from his post as Rector of the Panteios School of Political Sciences in Athens. With the fall of the military dictatorship in Greece, he returned to Athens and was nominated Governor of the National Bank of Greece.